Praise for *Who Will Accompany You?*

"Meg and her daughters' prose put me right there: trekking in Nepal or bouncing on the bus in remote Colombia. With humor and so much heart, this is more than a travel story; it's the story of letting go and watching your children fly."

—Kathleen Klofft, Travel Educator and Editor of GoSeeItTravel.com

"So profoundly moving, so beautifully crafted, so brave. This is a story about being true to oneself. Stafford brings all of herself to the reader as she shares her fears, doubts, triumphs, excitement, and love of life. This book is 100% authentic—because it is so human, so real."

—Susan Frankl, MD, Harvard Medical School

"A road map for parenting adventurous adults. Stafford asks all the right questions: Where are we headed in life? Who will come with us on the journey? How do we hold our children close while allowing them the freedom to grow? The most touching part: She doesn't hide the struggle as she tries (with love, curiosity, and humor) to find the answers."

—Fran Booth, LICSW Trainer, Internal Family Systems

"Meg is an accomplished therapist, memoirist, and organizational consultant. Now with *Who Will Accompany You?*, her second memoir, Meg illuminates how there may be no greater test in parenting than trekking around the globe with your adult daughters. While she will always be Mom, this is a delightful masterclass in auditioning one another as adult fellow travelers. A humor-filled and colorful triumph! The voices of Meg, Kate, and Gale are distinct, while their love, humor, and trust are the bungee cords holding these three together, supple and strong."

—**Mark Gianino**, PhD, MSW, Clinical Associate Professor,
Boston University School of Social Work

"I can't stop talking about this book! Its touching anecdotes and descriptions of unusual places keep finding their way into my conversation. From exotic or risky parts of the world, Meg Stafford's courageous daughters meld awareness, service, and international adventure at such young ages. Shepherded by the keen awareness of a mom who supports their global journeys, *Who Will Accompany You?* speaks to many angles of staying true to our own paths. I adore the rotating voices and perspectives of a mother and two daughters, woven together by a warm, golden thread of rich spirituality and love. This book will stay with you. Don't miss it."

—**Shawn Mahshie**, Thought Leader & Happiness
Coach, Author of *The Spark of Self-Love* and the upcoming
Self-Solidarity Solution

Who Will Accompany You?

MY MOTHER-DAUGHTER JOURNEYS,
FAR FROM HOME AND CLOSE TO THE HEART

MEG STAFFORD
with Kate Stafford and Gale Stafford

RIVER GROVE
BOOKS

Published by River Grove Books
Austin, TX
www.rivergrovebooks.com

Distributed by River Grove Books

Design and composition by Greenleaf Book Group and Kim Lance
Cover design by Greenleaf Book Group and Kim Lance

Publisher's Cataloging-in-Publication data is available.

Print ISBN: 978-1-63299-490-5

eBook ISBN: 978-1-63299-491-2

First Edition

To my mom, Sondra Sperber,
whose infectious love of travel brought us
closer together, no matter the distance

Contents

Preface

Certainly, travel is more than
the seeing of sights;
it is a change that goes on,
deep and permanent in the ideas of living.

—MARY RITTER BEARD

T HE WOMEN IN my family share a seemingly unquenchable craving for travel. What follows is not a recounting of how wanderlust gets passed from one generation to another passively, like blue eyes or the ability to curl your tongue. It's about how travel can affect our most significant relationships. I might even venture to say that travel has nudged my family's DNA.

When our first daughter was very young, my mom made her picture books based on the theme "Grandma Goes." Other grandparent-made gifts might focus on the reassuring idea that Grandma will always be a comforting presence at home. But Sondra was not that kind of grandma.

The travel bug manifested in her the summer I turned thirteen and my sister sixteen. She and my dad made their first European excursion then, a huge challenge for those of us left on the home front, and one that nearly caused my dear grandfather to disown us. As if to make up for lost time, she followed up with trips to China, England, Machu Picchu, Hawaii, Geneva, and Finland.

Years after my dad's death, my mom connected with a gentleman named Gene, who seemed to seek out travel as much as she did. In her early seventies, after a grand total of two dates, Sondra joined him for a decade of far-flung trips (Vietnam, Turkey, China, Australia, the Silk Road, and various parts of the States), punctuated by winters spent in San Miguel de Allende, Mexico, where Gene built a house. "Grandma Sure Did Go," leaving the Energizer Bunny in her wake.

My own itchy feet started at the age of four, when I took a shortcut to a friend's house, and I'm not sure that my mother was even aware of this little venture. My voyages continued for the next couple of decades. I was eager for every experience, and I had plenty of memorable ones: all-night dance parties in Besançon; the view of Mont-Saint-Michel at low tide; a 3 a.m. chocolate croissant in Aix-en-Provence; the saturated colors of an Albuquerque dawn; a night on my own in Vegas; hitchhiking to San Francisco.

Along the way, I met Pascal (a thrillingly cute French teenager); Mme. Renaud (an impossibly old woman who greeted our late-night returns to her Provençal home with a verbal flogging we could barely understand); an old man in wrinkled clothes who invited me to share coffee and doughnuts at a Southwestern truck stop ("You can do me more harm than I can do you," he pointed out); Wild Bill (a Bay Area college friend whose wee-hour banjo serenades convinced me it was time to move on); a roommate named Dave Harp (who meditated in the buff in our shared place in the Noe Valley); Phil, an English boyfriend (with whom I returned to Bristol); and a handsome roller-skating guy in LA who spent the entire day with me (I couldn't know then that Duke would become my husband someday).

And so my kids grew up seeing and hearing how life sometimes means taking risks, from sketchy bus trips, to unusual people, to the serious-looking scorpion we found in Gene's living room—after he'd sworn up and down that they'd never been a problem!

Risk is a part of life, of course, and everyone engages with it differently. The risks I encountered through travel prepared me for other, equally important kinds of risk: how to be vulnerable, how to be independent, how to love and be loved. And I like to think that my daughters understood that as well.

It should not have been surprising when both Gale and Kate decided to embark on their own large-scale adventures. We kept journals, wrote emails, talked through logistics, and ultimately tried to find meaning by reflecting on what we'd learned.

When I was first moved to combine the stories of our individual experiences, I wanted to compare our perspectives side by side, especially when it came to decision-making and how we nurtured the dynamic threads that united us.

Later, though, as I braided together our individual perspectives, I realized that travel had revealed something intriguing about how our relationships were evolving. Like the double-helix model, our intertwined spirals of connection and independence came to express our family's character and temperament.

The natural and expected tension that arises when separating from parents happens at all stages of growing up. One challenge for parents is recognizing and supporting children's choices and their ability to choose. As children become adults, and their decisions increasingly become wholly their own, how do we as parents know where to draw the line? My children's idiosyncratic choices invited me to grapple with that question over and over again.

We cannot control our children's environments completely, nor would most of us welcome that burden. One of the greatest gifts we can give our offspring is that of affording them simple choices early and often so that they can gain confidence in their own problem-solving.

I have tried as a parent to be respectful of the factors that go into those options, while mindfully guiding them when it seems important to do so. Not an easy formula. In the process of shaping this memoir, I found my children's choices during this period to be fascinating and sometimes terrifying, frustrating but ultimately inspiring my deep admiration.

I learned that—no matter how sound I may consider my own notions, theirs are certainly as good as or better, and that it is vital for them to listen to their own counsel. There is rarely one way to get somewhere, find something to eat, or discover something to do. If we're going somewhere on my nickel, I may offer up different choices than whatever they might allow. That's part of the fun. It's maybe not on their priority list to have a private bathroom or air conditioning, or to fly to an island to go scuba diving.

Probably the most fun for me is when my daughters or husband introduce me to new people, places, foods, or music. All my senses are in high receptor mode, ready to experience the new. I can totally focus, appreciating what's fresh or different. If they've already vetted something, I can be pretty certain I'll find it curious or captivating, but at the very least, interesting. (Butternut squash risotto with mushrooms, blue cheese, and fried bread crumbs? Bring it on!) It's the apex of awesome, regardless of my reaction. Well, wait a minute. It would not be terrific if

I spit out someone's newest creation. But that's the thing. We don't have to feel the exact same way. Just the willingness to give it a whirl is great in and of itself.

And trying something new together is a particular delight. It is a thrill to weigh their reactions, to compare responses, to note what the other appreciates—or even notices! What did you think of her accent in that film? Didn't you love Villanelle's outfits in *Killing Eve*? How does she make her character so charming and believable? Whether we agree or not, the love underneath is a constant, an unquestioning assumption (I freaking hope!), and a solid base for any exchange. It is the platform from which we can depart and return, the home base that tethers travel in the softest way.

My hope is that readers will see a bit of themselves, or a bit of possibility, in these pages.

For young adventurers, I hope our experiences fan your enthusiasm and remind you that there is so much to discover and embrace.

For parents, I hope our reflections help you know that you can be the air under your children's wings—even when clipping those wings might feel like the safer course of action.

Our priorities shift with life stage, but the desire for connection is a constant. Travel can be a symbol of the need to connect—to new places and people, to loved ones, and to ourselves. I am grateful for every interaction, and for the many ways in which our commonalities and differences create the spectacular quilt of life.

If we can be ongoing travelers—keeping our curiosity afloat, remaining open to learning, deferring control of the outcome of every situation—then we may find ourselves imbued with the beauty of every panorama, peak, and wave. From here to there, connected we go.

—Meg Stafford
Littleton, Massachusetts, 2021

Section One

Nepal and Bhutan, 2012

Miraculous turns of fate can happen to those
who persist in showing up.

—ELIZABETH GILBERT,
BIG MAGIC: CREATIVE LIVING BEYOND FEAR

MEG: During her senior year of high school, my younger daughter, Kate, told me she planned to travel to the Far East for a couple of weeks, to do research.

Following this adventure, she deferred, and ultimately abandoned, admission to Connecticut College in order to work and save money for a stint volunteering in South Africa.

A second round of work to fund a trip to New Zealand followed while awaiting acceptance to the University of Edinburgh, which was deemed to be more "centrally located."

Duke and I burst out laughing on hearing this declaration. Central? To what?

(What we couldn't have known then was that it would indeed be a convenient location from which to travel to a different European country each semester to visit friends or play Ultimate Frisbee with her team.)

Based on the above itinerary, you're probably envisioning Kate as something of a jet-setting risk-taker, the kid who's up for whatever, whenever. On the contrary, she approached these life-changing plans deliberately, methodically, and with consistent thoughtfulness.

From the beginning, Kate had the conviction of her beliefs. A shyish baby, she was not at all intimidated by having a more outgoing older sibling. Disdaining bottle feedings (feh!), she would wait for me to return from work to gain sustenance at the breast, as she preferred. On her second birthday, we realized she had learned how to exit her crib when we heard a thump from her room at the end of nap time. At three years old, she shimmied up the kitchen doorframe, so that when she called my name, I turned to find her at eye level.

Kate was a sight at the family camp we attended, hiking in her frilly skirt and the patent leather boots she'd pleaded for. She would enthusiastically participate in our Banathalon team (suffice it to say this is a relay race, the goal of which is to transport a banana from one part of the camp to another—via walking, paddling, swimming—before it's choked down on the race's final leg). She gradually transitioned to sleepaway camper and then to camp counselor.

Later, both our kids attended a public Charter Essential School, based on the principles of education giant Ted Sizer. The school embraced small classes, project-based learning, an emphasis on community, and the concept of student as learner and teacher as coach.

As she grew up, Kate was determined to challenge herself, but on her own terms. The tween who found Boston intimidating—and the rowdy Blue Man Group unbearable—later thought nothing of driving from our home in Massachusetts to Connecticut, Philadelphia, and

New York to see friends. Travel was a way of testing her boundaries and enlarging her scope.

Watching ideas crystallize as this seventeen-year-old planned her research trip to Asia was enlightening for me—as a traveler and a parent. In retrospect, it seems obvious that her vision was just a continuation of her previous path. But at the time, it was a challenge to see how this trip—and my role in the decision-making process—would fit into both our lives.

KATE: At my high school, senior projects are the big, final showcase of what you've learned. They aren't designed to highlight the content of your education. Rather, the projects are based on a topic of your choosing, showcasing the skills you've developed over the years: research, writing, and presentation, to name a few.

You work with an advisor to help find a topic you're really passionate about, something that you'll actually enjoy researching for an entire year. After you've come up with a topic, you receive feedback from the community (other students, parents, faculty), connecting you with others who may know about your topic or with sources you have yet to consider.

Happiness interested me generally (as has been the case for many others throughout history), but I chose to study it based on my growing interest in philosophy. In the time leading up to my senior year, I became increasingly passionate about the subject. Through feedback and preliminary research, I landed on studying happiness philosophically, psychologically (with a bit of hard neuroscience), and through the Buddhist lens. That seemed to be the best way to summarize one of the most-discussed topics of all time. We were encouraged to make experiential learning a part of the senior project, and I took that as my opportunity to find a way to travel.

MEG: Kate and I were hanging around the kitchen in the late afternoon, that easygoing time period before starting dinner and homework. She was relaxing in a padded chair as I cruised the cabinets in the vain hunt for undiscovered baked goods or chocolate.

"Hey, Mom, have I mentioned that . . ." This phrase was usually followed by something like, "I ran into Janey the other day. Haven't seen her in four years" or "I'm going to a party tomorrow night" or "I'm worried about Gerry. He hasn't been himself lately."

So I was unprepared for "I might go to Bhutan for my senior project."

I stuttered and spluttered like a parrot gone wild after nailing its first word: What? What? *What?*

And then: Bhutan? *Bhutan?* What?

I had been in "Sunday-afternoon-drive" mode before Kate yanked the wheel, stomped on the gas, and took us off-road into a bumpy passage somewhere in the Far East.

"Where exactly IS Bhutan?" I finally managed.

"Between India and China," she replied calmly.

Of course. Duh, who doesn't know that?

"How in the world did that come up?"

"Well, when the seniors presented their project ideas to the faculty and staff, several people asked me if I had looked into Bhutan."

She wasn't finished. "And Nancy, the school administrator, knows the king of Bhutan. In fact, she's going to his wedding next weekend and said she'd put in a word for me. She knows it'll be kind of busy there, but she hopes to speak with him."

This was really rich. "Nancy knows the *king* on a first-name basis?"

"Yeah," Kate responded. "He calls her his American mom."

Sure he does. But I was still not getting it. "So what does Bhutan have to do with your project?"

"Well, it turns out that they measure the success of the country by how happy the people are."

Now she had my attention. "Really? I wonder how they actually measure it?" We were to learn later that the population responds via survey. But in some ways it really didn't matter. The fact that they were measuring *any* kind of happiness, no matter how it was defined, was fascinating enough.

"They don't really encourage tourism, but if I went there, they would make time for me and show me around."

I had to admit, I was torn between packing my own bags and completely forbidding any teenage foray to somewhere so far away. Fortunately, we had time to digest the whole concept, as Nancy would be out of the country for the next couple of weeks, and therefore no concrete plans would be brought up before then.

I understood the notion of this kind of travel. After all, I turned fifteen in France, when I tagged along with a friend and her parents, who had chaperoned a college trip. When I was sixteen, much to my irritation, my parents would not allow me to go to Greece with friends the following year, and I didn't get there until I was twenty-six. As a solo venture, it was quite the challenge, but my wanderlust was firmly in place when I was Kate's age.

Kate's plan was a bit more unsettling, but if there were solid arrangements, I would be hard-pressed to oppose it. She was used to being away from home; that part didn't worry me. But she had not traveled alone, and certainly not to the other side of the world.

Months later, my husband Duke and I were having brunch with friends when one of them asked if we had simply considered saying no. I stared at him as though he had asked whether we would wrap our child in chains of spaghetti. Then I burst out laughing. Of the many responses I struggled with, that seemed to be the only one that had not even crossed my mind! It was never a matter of whether she would go, but how and under what circumstances.

Regardless of what came of Kate's idea, I realized that I was proud that she had the confidence to consider the risk and to pursue her interests and dreams out in the vast and varied world.

And the next time she casually asked whether she had mentioned something, I would fasten my seatbelt and prepare for the ride.

When Kate did get in touch with the Minister of the GNH (Gross National Happiness—yes, really), it was only to learn that there was a significant daily tax for tourists (around $300 per person). A stay of several weeks was out of the question.

Her mentor for her project, a Buddhist nun, mentioned that monasteries in Nepal and India offered reasonably priced beginner programs. We did not take Kate seriously until the beginning of January, when she announced her new plan, including a week in each country and about a week in between, complete with dates and a tentative itinerary.

The adventure had all been abstract—an idea, a possibility, a dream—until now. Suddenly it had wings and a destination.

It took a bit of soul searching and consultation with others to realize that Duke and I were not comfortable with Kate's making this a solo venture.

The solution? I would accompany her as far as Kopan Monastery in Nepal and then organize a trek to the Annapurna Base Camp, at 14,000 feet, for myself and my friend Lisa, who was living temporarily in Hong Kong.

Afterward, Lisa would return home, while Kate and I would reconnect in Kathmandu and then spend three days in Bhutan. All the pieces had to be put into place for a trip that was to begin in just over a month.

It had once been my habit to travel for extended periods, but I had not been away for more than a week in the past twenty-five years. I tingled with excitement about both my trek to the Annapurna Sanctuary and travel with Kate. While we raced to finalize our plans, I hoped she understood that most of the adventures awaiting her would not include a hiking-boot-toting mama. But for now, the unknown beckoned, opening its arms and inviting us to revel in its mysteries. Exploring it together meant that we could absorb the expanse of possibilities that Nepal and Bhutan could serve up in three weeks from the safety of our connection.

The only hesitation came from my bank account, which tapped me on the shoulder, slapped the back of my head, and hissed, "What are you thinking? You're about to embark on another set of college payments!"

"Hush," I fired back. "We'll figure that out. Gotta jump on this adventure while I can still catch the train."

KATE: *Journal excerpt,* 1/1/2012: The author Gretchen Rubin (and Buddhism, basically) says that removing negativity from one's life creates the biggest increase in happiness (unsurprisingly). For me, putting things off is the largest negative force in my life. I've decided to adopt a "do it now" philosophy as my resolution, and I will hold myself accountable in this journal.

KATE: *Journal excerpt*, 2/10/2012: I haven't journaled in over a month. But other than that, I've been doing better with my "do it now" resolution, which speaks to both psychological and Buddhist happiness philosophies.

I had a conversation with my mom about Dan Gilbert's theory of happiness, that the best way to predict happiness is to follow the example of someone who is currently where you will be in the future. She made the case that I follow this philosophy very deeply to make my decisions. I look to the people I respect, who are currently in the situations I will soon be in, and base my future on this. I hadn't even considered the fact that I do this; it is my natural inclination and generally works for me.

Is choosing a college different from choosing what I'll eat for lunch? Can a race car driver assume what movie an accountant will enjoy? And do all these questions arise from the fact that I believe, and want to believe, that I and all other people are unique?

KATE: *Journal excerpt*, 2/22/12: I am on a twelve-hour flight from JFK Airport in New York to Dubai in the United Arab Emirates! Buildup is important to happiness. I have been enjoying the anticipation of this trip, and now it's finally here.

I have been reflecting on health and wealth. Reading *Eat, Pray, Love* by Elizabeth Gilbert, I came across the Italian phrase *"il bel far niente,"* meaning "the beauty of doing nothing." I love this and completely see its relevance. I wish this idea were better accepted in our society, where ambition is a double-edged sword. I wish we could see *"il bel far niente,"* instead of "lazy."

I reflected on how culture changes our perceptions of happiness. I am two hours and twenty-one minutes away from countries that may have entirely different ideas of happiness.

I'm so tired and also so grateful for this trip. The more you put out for happiness, the more you receive. Challenge is key. I am tapping into this big-time and hoping for an equally big payoff. But if not, I'm sure I'll still learn something.

MEG: "Find the hospital," a colleague had advised when she learned of my plans. "You'll need it, because everyone gets sick. Stay away from avalanches, particularly at the base camp and where there are open fields."

These admonitions had receded into the depths of my mind as the lights of the Kathmandu Valley twinkled in the early-evening light, and a shiver of excitement kept us from feeling the fatigue of our journey of more than twenty-four hours. The other passengers on our flight comprised the only people in the terminal, and we were lulled into believing that we had arrived at a small provincial airport. Obtaining a visa meant filling out a short form and producing forty dollars in cash. Carrying our duffel bags, we were waved through customs, past a score of men offering taxi rides, to our first glimpse of the outdoors.

Night had crept in during our brief time in the airport, abruptly reminding me that we had indeed traveled a long way. I searched the jumble of greeters in dark clothing and cars. We were clearly the only Western mother/daughter pair among the arriving travelers. Then I spotted the sign—"Grand Asian Journeys"—held by a man who was searching for our faces as anxiously as we were seeking his. For once, I appreciated that we looked like tourists.

"Meg and Kate?" Ram asked, looking relieved. He introduced our driver as they heaped our bags into the trunk of a waiting car.

I hadn't realized that the Nepalese drive on the left and was momentarily disoriented. But as we exited the airport, the only obvious conclusion was that we would never make it to the hotel. I could see no safe way to navigate the surge of cars, people, bikes, and unflappable cows that populated the streets. Our driver seemed unconcerned as he swerved around pedestrians, tooting the horn while rounding corners that were too narrow for more than one car—which was all of them. The maze ended, somehow, at our hotel.

Exhausted, we managed some sleep. We were ravenous upon awakening and fell upon a buffet of bread, yogurt, fruit, cereal, juice, coffee, and tea. We pondered which foods were safe to eat. Anything we could peel or heat got a thumbs-up, as did anything in a box or a can. Only after stuffing ourselves with oranges, grapefruit, cereal, and toast did we realize that my friend Lisa—looking relaxed and part of the scene—was sitting behind us at her own table in a sunny spot.

Our driver took the three of us out of the chaotic city, onto the highway, and past rows of shops arranged like an outdoor mall. We parked near a wooded area and walked toward the Bagmati, a holy river.

This was an area clearly designed for tourists. A man was hawking charming stringed instruments in the form of hollowed-out gourds, his gaze frank and open, with some expectation that we would engage.

I realized that he needed to be somewhat aggressive to make sales, but I was too freshly off the plane to invest in either a discussion or a purchase. I am always taken by musical instruments, but I was reluctant to acquire things that would weigh me down so early in our travels. We both settled for a photograph.

Women were selling dyeing materials in gorgeous, intense hues of magenta, gold, turquoise, red, navy, and lime green. Lined up in rectangular blocks, the bold saturation of color struck a sharp contrast to the dreariness—at least as perceived by my Western eyes—of the scene just beyond.

Our guide had brought us to this picturesque spot because it's also a culturally important site. He explained that people brought their dying relatives here and cared for them in a building set back several yards from the river.

We climbed up the hillside opposite. From the benches there, we could watch people performing a pre-death ritual across the river without disturbing them.

I imagined that it must be a comfort in being brought to this holy place when death was imminent, but it was a cultural stretch for me to see people swimming or bathing in the river so close to others keeping vigil with their families. These activities are so completely separated in our culture.

It was challenging to put my assumptions aside and not feel voyeuristic.

The vast majority of the Nepalese people—about 81 percent—are Hindu, 9 percent Buddhist, 4.4 percent Muslim, and the remainder Kiratist, Christian, Sikh, and others. Religious beliefs here seemed woven into the culture, and I became aware of them in a way I never would have noticed in the United States.

Monkeys scattered around the area across the river from the

temple, but Lisa, well versed in monkey shenanigans, was not in the least charmed by them.

"Be careful," she warned. "They'll grab food or whatever you're holding and run away with it. They may look cute, but trust me, that doesn't last. A camera is as amusing to grab as a handkerchief to them."

Because Lisa is not one to be frivolous with words, I tried to be wary of these adorable creatures. Their unself-conscious curiosity was so appealing; how could they beguile us?

I had promised Duke that I would bring him a metal singing bowl, so after our visit to the Bagmati, we traveled with our guide to visit a shop in Patan where they are made.

The owner chose one and demonstrated how striking its side makes one tone, while running the mallet along the outside sets up a harmonic. The ethereal, ancient sound filled the room, emanating from everywhere at once. It filled the hollows in our souls, taking us back thousands of years, connecting us to its maker. He filled the bowl with water, which danced in sparkling, dynamic fountains as the vibrations from the mallet along the rim set it into motion.

Next, he flipped it upside down and instructed us each in turn to place the bowl on our heads (as if we were sporting World War II helmets). When he struck it, we received the healing vibrations that resulted.

"Since humans are about 60 percent water," he informed us, "our bodies respond to the vibrations whether we are attempting to or not." With our thumbs and index fingers touching and placed on our knees, we could sense the meaning of his words.

He recommended a particular bowl for me to bring home, and I was thrilled to buy it. I had to take him at his word, because I had no means by which to judge for myself. Years later, though, when I brought our quartet of singing bowls to my yoga teacher, she was immediately drawn to the one I had bought in Nepal. This one, she intoned, was very special.

Kate reaping the benefits of the vibrations of the singing bowl.

KATE: *Journal excerpt, 2/23, bedtime:* The trip is definitely real now. Kathmandu is different from anything I've ever seen. The air is dirty, there are people everywhere, and the buildings are old and broken down. Because of power shortages, there are blackouts every once in a while. It's a little shady, but so full of life. I've never been around so much poverty all in one place. The upscale parts of the city cater strictly to Westerners.

Our guide, Jwalant, is thirty-six years old and very polite. He lives in the same house he grew up in, with his parents (he takes care of them, a common arrangement here). After attending college in Seattle, he returned to Nepal. Although he liked his experience in the States, he told us, "Life is better here." He couldn't imagine waking up every day to go to work for someone else, only to go home, go to bed, and do it again the next day.

Happiness is so much about perspective and priorities. He is happier here, in a city I perceive as hectic and dirty, leading a lifestyle very different from what he kept referring to as "Corporate America." Another argument for why we can't tell other people whether they're happy or not.

MEG: After the day of touring, we deposited Kate at Kopan Monastery, where she would study meditation and Tibetan Buddhism for the next twelve days.

The monastery sits on a hill on the outskirts of town, and we wound our way up the narrow streets in the old car driven by our guide. Once again, I reminded myself that I needed to trust that we would get where we were going without falling off the side of the road, breaking down, or taking out a crowd of people (or cows). It would have been really bad form to crush the people of our host country—or the animals that are their honored guests.

Kopan turned out to be orderly and organized. It was a relief to know that they were expecting Kate and had a room for her. We didn't linger long, as there was nothing I could do to make this transition any easier.

My tummy did a few flip-flops as we took in the expansive view of the valley while descending the curvy, poorly paved road. I thought about Kate's next few hours and took some deep breaths. I sent her love, calm, and wishes for an informative and satisfying stay.

Meeting people would be crucial for Kate; she would have a hard time connecting with the program if she did not feel included in the group. She was good at making connections, but it would still be a challenge, particularly with the first half of the day taking place in silence. There would be gaps before she could be in tune with the other people there, and then there would be the inevitable leap across the gap. There is no other way.

She had done it before and probably would not even realize that she was doing it again. Taking things as they came and going with the flow of the day would lead her to the people she needed to meet.

I was accustomed to Kate's being away from home, but her summer camp was just a two-hour drive from home. Now she would be several days' hike and a flight away. We were both ready for this experience, but, while excited, I found myself unprepared.

My family had been the mainstay and focus of my life. I loved being a mother: the errands together, the transporting, the time spent cooking and eating together, talking about our day, visiting relatives. It was a way of life that was so very pleasing and natural, made all the more so by my vast enjoyment of the people with whom I was living.

We were not without our differences, of course. Both girls pushed the limits of independence, which at once gratified and challenged me.

There were arguments. Kate was once incensed when we forbade her from driving on icy roads to visit friends a couple of towns away, and despite her confidence, we would not budge. After a college discussion turned out badly, Gale stomped off and walked to a friend's house—twelve miles away. Can't fault our girls for a lack of strong opinions, wherever that came from.

In retrospect, it was a good thing that they were away from home at different times (mostly). However, there was a time when Gale was in Colombia while Kate was in New Zealand—and we couldn't get in touch with either one of them. Our family relied then on the ethereal connection of the internet, and we had to have faith that our relationships were continuing to grow, even across distance and time.

Although we were not in the same place, we sure as hell had a lot to talk about. I always wanted to know more about their experiences, who they were meeting, and what they found interesting, challenging, surprising, remarkable.

While email is no substitute for being together, I could not possibly hold back the reins when their spirits were spurring them on toward adventure. It was our job as parents to be ready to receive them when they had questions, needed a touch of home, or wanted to hear a familiar voice. It could not be on our schedule. It had to be when they were ready, when they needed to be in touch.

Waiting has never been my long suit. For instance, I want to be good at sports right away, to know the dance moves, to be able to do all the yoga poses. But I was never going to be great at yoga right off the bat. My body couldn't immediately access the necessary flexibility, balance, and strength. I had to learn to be content with breathing and progressing slowly, over time. I could do a backbend easily as a kid, so I knew it was possible. It took some doing, but I was able to achieve it after several months as an adult student. Other poses took much longer. And some I can only hope to come close to.

Patience with other people, my kids included, is different. I can recalibrate when I'm waiting for others. Mostly.

KATE: *Journal excerpt,* 2/24: While the monks at Kopan intimidate me, I do realize that they're modern. I'll see a monk walking around the monastery, with shaved head and traditional dress, and then see him answer his smartphone!

The monks are of all ages, but the youngest are boys of about five years old. It made me think about choosing one's own path to happiness. The little boys didn't choose to be monks. If a person is placed on a path to happiness, how do they know that one is best? Or is it the same as someone choosing a path? Are our brains equipped to make us believe the path we're on is the best path? I'm not sure, but it's something to think on.

I am especially impressed with Western people who choose to live an entirely Buddhist life. I find it even more difficult to imagine giving up my life at home for the life of a monk.

I'm in an odd limbo. I haven't started meditating, and I won't until Sunday night. It is Friday night now, and I'm not sure how I'm going to fill my Saturday. I plan a lot of exploring and reading.

I'm really leaning on the theories that meditation brings happiness and that challenge brings happiness. This is the most risky and challenging thing I have ever done.

Upon arriving at Kopan I was thrilled—and also more terrified than I remember being in a long time. I felt so lonely and realized that I have no idea what I'm doing, and that's scary. I couldn't seem to find my footing, and it still feels that way a little bit.

After a very lonely dinner, I helped do the dishes. I talked to a German man named Oshram, and he told me that there was nothing to be worried about, as the course would be boring. I like to hear that. "Boring" is something I can handle. Washing the thin tin dishes calmed me. I felt like I belonged, and I was able to clear my mind for a while.

KATE: *Journal excerpt, 2/25:* I'm in a new place, with lots of sounds and unfamiliarities, but I believe the reason I got only an OK night's sleep is that I am very alone. I am more alone than I have been in my entire life. I'm away from my family, house, country, and everything I know. Being alone is not a bad thing at a Buddhist retreat; it allows me to be alone with my thoughts and mind, which is basically the point.

But it's terrifying. Without a safety net, being with my thoughts is incredibly scary.

I think I'll be OK, though. Oshram said that many people come in with doubts, and most end up liking it. I'm coming in with an open mind, so I should definitely be OK, right? I told him a little bit about my project, and he said, "Well, they talk a lot about happiness here." At least I'm in the right place.

KATE: *Journal excerpt, 2/26:* People are so sweet and gentle, and I met a couple more today. Soo from Hong Kong sat down and had breakfast with me. She travels a lot (but doesn't call it travel) and is scattered and outgoing (but doesn't call it outgoing).

Michael from England found me as I was taking pictures of a beautiful statue. He told me I was brave for coming here so young. I told
him I'm naive.

This is why I traveled so far to take a course on Buddhism. I could
take one at home, but I wouldn't have had the incredible experience of
meeting extraordinary people from across the globe. The overwhelming sense of fulfillment I get from meeting them is what I would call
happiness, the deep, virtuous kind that Aristotle recommends. Soo says
the kind of people that come to these things are just an "all right group
of people." I think she's right.

I just had a great time going down to the village of Boudha with
Michael, Ross and Jordan from Australia, and Thomas from Denmark.
I spoke with Michael about my project, and happiness. He said more
and more people are coming to Buddhism and similar practices because
more and more people are asking themselves whether they're truly
happy—and finding out that they can't answer, because they don't know
what true happiness is. I like to believe that people can define for themselves what happiness is (for the most part). It feels like a contradiction
to be open minded, but then to put happiness into one small bubble.

MEG: I have known Lisa, my travel buddy, for several years. We met
in a group studying executive coaching, but we had never so much as
enjoyed a cup of coffee together before now.

Lisa is an esteemed nutritionist by trade, and a dancer at heart, with
a specialty in a dance/yoga style called Nia. Light and lithe, she was
coming from a three-week hiking trip in New Zealand with her own
daughter and had not had time to bone up on local customs. Unaware

that women do not show their legs in Nepal, she told me that she felt assaulted by the intensity of the male gaze on her arrival.

I learned that her father was paralyzed in a plane crash months after she was born. Because he was home for much of her early upbringing, her experiences were significantly different than those of her nine older siblings.

"My parents didn't want me to go to medical school," she recalled. "Nutrition and eating healthy were extremely important to my mother from very early on, and it is not a coincidence that I became a nutritionist."

After our second day of touring, we dined with a new contact of hers (the connection was made via a Hong Kong friend in the clothing business) who owns a shop in Kathmandu. Yasmine's mother is French and Greek, and her father is Berber. Born in Germany and raised in Morocco, she now lives part time in Kathmandu and part time in New York City, where she attended the Fashion Institute of Technology. Her cosmopolitan background made my head spin, and I wondered how long it would take me to learn half the languages she spoke.

Yasmine explained that she wanted women to feel good in their clothing and to feel connected to her, the designer. I told her I hoped to be able to visit her shop to see how her unique, colorful style reflects the blend of cultures in which she's lived.

The restaurant was lit mostly by candlelight. The capricious electricity cut out shortly after our arrival and did not blink back on until we were finishing our meal, which is typical for this overloaded city.

People migrate from the valley into Kathmandu in hopes of finding greater opportunity, and their numbers overwhelm the existing infrastructure in every way. How many years would it take for the supply of electricity to catch up with the demand? At the time of our visit, people had learned to share the power supply—and everyone had a backup plan.

After dinner, Lisa and I carefully packed our bags with what was absolutely necessary for the trek, leaving behind the few items that would remain clean for the next ten days. At the recommendation of our tour organizer, we used Ziploc bags to keep items separate and dry, a technique that was to serve its purpose over and over.

At 1 a.m. my stomach started to rumble, as my usual ironclad system reacted to something unfamiliar. Fortunately, my uncharacteristically crowded bag of pharmaceutical remedies held a bottle of PB (Pepto-Bismol, not peanut butter), but I still spent my first night with my new roommate draped unceremoniously around the porcelain bowl. I hoped that Lisa was not already regretting her decision to accompany me on this little escapade to 14,000 feet.

It turned out that the culprit was probably my Invisalign braces. Careful as I had been to drink only bottled water, I had washed the removable braces in tap water, which was enough to cause my abdominal distress. I made that mistake only once, but it was a rookie move. Of all times to be sporting these "convenient" teeth shifters.

(Years later, Lisa told me that she had worried that I would be sick for the entire trip. I, on the other hand, was certain that my appetite would return to its usual substantial demand in a day or two.)

Altitude was also a concern, as Lisa had had an adverse reaction in the past. We both came equipped with medication to mitigate the effects, but our tour organizer Jwalant was a proponent of gradual adjustment. We would ascend in six days and descend in four, taking the extra time to be gentle to our bodies.

Lila, our guide for the hiking portion, had traveled from the eastern part of Nepal to meet us at the Kathmandu airport, facilitating the arrangements for our hour-long flight to Pokhara. (Because of the steepness of the mountains and state of the roads, the trip would have taken twenty-four hours by bus.) We were weighed and assigned seats in the ten-seater. I looked balefully out the window, still feeling unwell. Small planes are my favorite, and this would otherwise have been a highlight of the journey. In the end, I was grateful that the short but dramatic flight over the rugged mountains was uneventful—although I did worry that my stomach would share whatever semi-digested contents remained.

Lila was a compact, fifty-something, taciturn man who had learned English from accompanying other visitors. Early on, he mentioned Machapuchare, describing the mountain in a way we finally understood to mean "fishtail." When it came into view at last, it looked like a child's drawing, with the route winding around it.

He set a steady pace and never seemed hurried in any way. In contrast to his gradual, smooth stride, I felt like I was scrambling. Lisa was quicker on the uphill, and I didn't want to be a laggard.

Lila was protective of us in a quiet, understated way. He insisted that I get a sun hat, and I grabbed a cap with "Bob" written on the front. Our huge Maine coon cat back home is called Bob(cat), and my brother-in-law is Bob. It felt good to be reminded of both of them.

Lila also gifted me with a bamboo pole to use as a walking stick, in order to reduce leg stress. I had never used one in my many years of hiking, but I quickly realized its value. (This knowledge did not stop me from regularly forgetting my trusty staff, but Lila made sure I retrieved it every time.)

Having done this route several times before, Lila was constantly reassuring us that we didn't need to hurry, that we were doing fine. He was even (mostly) patient with our picture-taking and ongoing fascination with waterfalls.

During lunch on the first day of our trek, we ran into people who had literally been fleeing from an avalanche. An animated woman with wild eyes described how she had been running to keep ahead of it, and her husband shouted that he had been hit in the back by flying debris. It was that close.

I listened with only half an ear, because I was still feeling wretched. It was all I could do to choke down a hardboiled egg so I would have some modicum of energy for the next couple hours of hiking. Perhaps this was just as well, because the notion of being buried alive gave me the gugs. (At this point, I admit that I recalled my colleague's pre-trip advice about avoiding avalanches a bit more seriously.)

Lisa had her own reaction to the couple's anxiety. A short while after talking to them, she noticed a helicopter filled with people all dressed alike. She recalled the animated woman mentioning how a Korean group had to be airlifted out of the area.

We either had to turn back or trust in our guide's expertise. Lila assured us that we would be taking an entirely different route, on the other side of the mountain.

And so we decided to continue. Kate was not the only one who needed to make a leap of faith.

After a couple of hours, we arrived at Nyapul. The lodge was just off the path, with no other dwellings in the vicinity but great views all around.

Lisa suggested that we get separate rooms if there was an extra one available. It was early in the trekking season, so this was easily accommodated.

Only when I'm really down for the count do I need sleep during the day, but evidently this was one of those times. I awoke feeling better. The bathrooms were across the courtyard, and of the hole-in-the-ground variety in stalls, and I sent up a prayer that I would not need to spend copious amounts of time there.

Cipro, Imodium, and charcoal made a powerful cocktail, and I was grateful for the pharmacy I was lugging around with me. Gotta keep up with the probiotics, amateurbiotics, anti- and uncle-biotics—the entire Biotics clan.

I hoped the primitive shower would be available, but nope. It would have to wait until after dinner. At least there was one. Showers were by no means guaranteed, and neither was hot water. At least I would be able to wash away my upset feeling before we headed off in the morning. After more eggs for dinner, we retired to our rooms. Breakfast would be at eight, with departure soon after.

The habit of retiring soon after dinner would become routine. We were typically tired from several hours of trekking, and there was of course no distraction in the form of chores, phone calls, or work of any type. We were left with our thoughts, our books and journals, and the empty space to feel full.

What a luxury to inhale the pattern of the mountains sloping toward one another, to see them in the distance, ever lighter shades of blue until the last one faded into the sky surrounding it. So calm and reassuring. Their deep presence, and the enormity of scale, provided a feeling of safety and of being encompassed by a loving essence.

Lila collected our water bottles and filled them with boiled water each morning before we set off, careful of our Western stomachs. I was unaccustomed to having someone look after me in this mother-hen kind of way and appreciated his care, although I found it a little embarrassing.

Whenever we were at a lodge with electricity, we plugged in our phones. Inevitably, Lila would appear from nowhere, admonishing, "You stay with phone."

We were always eager to avail ourselves of showers, if there were any (especially in the early, unexpectedly warm part of the trip), and couldn't be bothered to babysit our electronics. We were casual (read: overtrusting) with our devices and assumed that the absence of other humans was license to let them charge unattended.

Lila's gentle stubbornness allowed me to feel like a teenager protected by a loving parent. I was usually the organizer of my family's trips, and having someone else doing the reminding and caretaking instead took me aback.

When we arrived in Chomrong, we headed back downhill to the one shop that offered internet access. On our way, we passed a school with "Patience, Calmness, and Curiousness" written above the doorways.

A young man wearing white pants, a black jacket, and a cap shaped like a fez smiled and said hello in English. Harry was a teacher at the school. We chatted briefly, and he confirmed that indeed we were on the right path to the shop.

We asked to take his photograph, and he struck a proud pose. He asked us to take another one, and this time he gave a sideways peace sign and cocked his head to one side. For the next photo, he unzipped his jacket, revealing a gleaming white T-shirt beneath. He planted his hands on his hips and smiled like James Dean. Next, I took a shot of Lisa smiling next to him. "Do we make a nice couple?" she asked, inclining her head toward him.

It was late February, still early in the trekking season, and almost no one else was staying in Chomrong. In fact, for the first few nights, there were only a handful of other guests, and Lisa and I had a virtually private dinner. I tried to imagine what it would be like with all the lodges filled. Much more lively and loud, more competition for the showers and power outlets. I could imagine the fun of hanging out with other people from who-knows-where. In contrast, our visit was rather meditative.

After dinner we noticed a bunch of teenagers dancing to music. A fellow English speaker explained that Muslim and Hindu school groups were getting to know each other. We stayed for a little while, appreciative of this venture and how it must be for them to forge relationships with one another, before sleep beckoned us back to our lodging.

It made perfect sense to gather these groups, surrounded by the comforting hug of the enormous mountains that have stood for millennia, impervious to differences between nations, religions, and patterns of thought. The challenges are the same for all people. Everyone gets cold, tired, hungry, and enamored of the evolving views surrounding them. The mountains keep everyone's secrets, their fears, their triumphs. They protect and challenge us all.

In the morning as we began our daily trek, Lisa gently teased Lila. "I saw you dancing out there, Lila. It looked like you were having a great time."

"Oh, no, I was not dancing," he declared with certainty. He looked stricken and emphasized seriously, "No, not dancing. No, no."

"Oh yeah, I saw you out there," Lisa insisted, grinning. "You were moving right along there."

"No, was not. No dancing." Lila was adamant, and I could feel his anxiety. I tried to give her the universal "cut it out" sign, slashing an open outstretched hand across my throat. She saw me and gave one more try: "Oh, come on, Lila. It's OK." He did not respond, and she let it drop.

It was obvious—to me—that Lisa was joking. But it was just as plain that to Lila, this was a serious matter. He could not read her playful expression or manner. It would have been funny if he hadn't seemed so literal and upset about the whole affair.

Joking is not simple. Tragedy is the same in any language, but humor does not translate so easily. I hadn't seen it play out quite so graphically until then. Maybe Lila thought he was being accused of doing something wrong.

Our porter, Amar, was a slim, trim, spring-loaded twenty-four-year-old. Despite the outsized, almost comically large pack strapped around his forehead, he bounded up and down the peaks. He was usually well rested by the time we showed up. He was like the Road Runner, leaving us in his dust as we plodded along.

I was convinced he had martial arts training, as I had caught him sometimes leaping in the air when he thought no one was watching. It was inspiring to behold how he achieved breathtaking height with seemingly minimal effort, given my own huffing and puffing under the weight of only my little day pack. I sent up my gratitude many times a day for his stamina.

One day he was singing the most beautiful, haunting tune, a musical feast exquisitely fitted to the setting. I realized that I had probably missed days of this music, because he was almost always so far ahead of us. I was able to record some of it, making his musical accompaniment to our journey available for posterity.

KATE: *Journal excerpt,* 2/26, 6:35 *a.m.:* I had my first full meditation last night! I meditated for an hour, completely unguided. It was the first time I meditated that long on my own. I'm so incredibly proud, and I felt great afterward. Coming out of a meditation that long feels like having had a combination of a perfect nap and stimulating conversation.

Of course it wasn't easy, but I was happy to find out that Michael and Thomas found it difficult as well. Their minds also wandered, wondering how much time was left. Time moves strangely at Kopan, as it does in meditation, when all sense of time is just dissolved. You can't tell if it's been a minute or an hour. I've only been here for a day and a half, and it feels like forever. The others say they feel that way too.

I'm so glad I did the meditation yesterday, because now I know I can do it during the course, which starts today! I believe the longest meditation will be an hour, and I've already done that.

I spent a long time talking and walking around Kopan last night with Daniel, who is from India/Australia and who arrived yesterday. It was nice to connect with someone of about the same age. While so many people came here for an independent journey (what I was expecting), so much of the experience turns out to include conversation. I absolutely love being in a place with people from all over the world.

KATE: *Journal excerpt,* 2/27, 5:25 *a.m.:* My entry was cut short yesterday, because I left to meditate with Michael and Thomas. As before, our half hour felt much longer. Then I didn't get back to the room last night until 9:45 p.m., and I wanted to get as much sleep as I could before waking up at 5 a.m. Everyone talks about their sleep being weird, and mine is no exception.

I had had no down time during the day, because I got lost in Kathmandu with Daniel and my new friend Manja, from Germany. The three of us seem like the youngest students at Kopan, so we stick together and have become fast friends. We agreed that's what happens when you travel. That sense of immediate belonging is hard to find at home.

Daniel and I decided to accompany Manja to get her visa extended. We were having a lovely time getting to know each other. Manja went to a cyber cafe, and we agreed to meet in an hour.

Daniel and I walked around Durbar Square and Freak Street, just wandering. In an hour, we were completely lost. But we worked it out and ended up being only five minutes late. I was so proud and excited! I never freaked out, even though I was lost in a foreign city. The three of us ate momos and delicious chocolate cake, bought pants to meditate in, and headed home.

Our bus completely overshot our destination, and so we had to take another bus, and then a taxi. We missed the first tea as a group and the first introductory session—and we almost missed dinner!

But I was unbothered. I got to see incredible, beautiful parts of Nepal that I would otherwise never have seen. I couldn't change the situation, so there was no point in getting upset about it. And I ended up having a wonderful time.

The first session with Ven Palzang, the teacher of the course, was great. Even with one hundred people, he made it seem personal. He is very friendly and even (of course), and he has a sense of humor. He makes Buddhism accessible.

Today will be a long day, starting early (I guess that will be true for every day!). This will be the first day of sitting through meditations and teachings. And the sitting is the hardest part.

KATE: *Journal excerpt,* 2/27, 8:20 *a.m.:* I have some downtime before the next teaching. Silence really does force you to spend time with only yourself. You can physically be around other people, but it means nothing if you can't communicate with such a friendly group of people. I don't mind the silence. But honestly, I hope that people do talk after lunch, once we're allowed to.

The first formal meditation was this morning. Ven Palzang's assistant offered us a few words before sending us off to meditate.

There are two different forms of meditation. The first, what we're doing this morning, is focusing your mind on a single thing—generally an image of Buddha or your breathing—for the totality of the meditation. This is very different from the constant shifting from topic to topic that your brain usually does.

(Ironically, I just took a short pause to walk to the animal sanctuary with Daniel to see the goats. So cute!)

This focus helps you live in the moment, instead of always jumping to the next thing (solving the problem of people failing to predict the future, as author Elizabeth Gilbert points out, as you can't be disappointed if you have no expectations). This is one of the reasons we're in silence. With fewer distractions, it's easier to focus on the present.

I know less about the other type of meditation, which is called analytical, but my understanding is that we must constantly ask ourselves why and look for our motivation before every session.

I was hesitant about keeping a journal as part of my project, because I wanted to study happiness as a whole, not my own personal happiness. But here, after every session, we dedicate the positive karma we've earned to someone. And as this is the Buddhist philosophy, we dedicate it to all sentient beings. I feel that doing this journal, this course, this project is all for something larger than myself, and I truly appreciate that.

MEG: I'm experiencing a moment of intense appreciation for the privilege of being in these majestic mountains, spending a little bit of time with the people of these remote places.

Our lives are of equal importance, but we are so very different from one another. We all have families; we all need to eat and shelter from the elements. But what are their aspirations, hopes, dreams? What is important to them? What do they think about at night, or in that in-between time before being fully awake? Do they ponder what other parts of Nepal are like? Do they visit people in the larger towns or cities? What are their relationships like? Tibetan prayer flags flutter as the breeze lifts the light fabric. They are a moving backdrop, an homage to a deeper part of the people here, their community, and their beliefs.

We seemed to be the only tourists here, which is both odd and relaxing. Lila took our orders, and we ate maybe an hour later. I was just starting to be adventurous in my food choices again.

We watched *Water for Elephants* on my iPad. How incredibly fortunate to tote around this piece of equipment that allows us to watch a movie so far from anywhere movies are shown! I purchased it for the flights, but in addition to its entertainment value, it's turned into the perfect compact writing tool. Afterward, to bed at ten, up at six, with one melatonin break to help me get back to sleep.

It was striking how important it had become to race to the internet when I could—to reassure Duke, Gale, and my mom that things were fine, but also to connect. My intent in being here had nothing to do with "getting away." Rather, I wanted to enjoy the profundity of the mountains and learn about the place.

In the deep stillness, I pondered the concept of connecting the spirit to the soul. I was not certain what that means or how it shows up. This kind of travel—being close to the land, walking on it, observing the mountains, being a part of this place, so vast and different—filled me in a way that nothing else does.

I could focus on this day, this moment, this connection to everything around me *right now*. It is so rooted in my core, and yet I had not been feeding this part of myself for a long time. There were lots of good reasons for that, and I didn't resent them, but I soaked up a feeling of homecoming like rain after a drought.

We made a remarkable discovery: Popcorn was on the menu. Ordering something so predictable, so seemingly American, felt a little like cheating. We expected it to arrive packaged and coated with cheesy chemicals, but it turned out to be made fresh, an incredible treat!

Of all the things to remind me of home, I would not have expected this to be one. Duke, the popcorn pro, knows to give me my own bowl so that I don't scarf down everyone else's. Many a football game has been saved by this tactic. But here, on the other side of the world, at 2,170 meters, I was happy to share.

I was particularly fond of the many signs we passed along the way, and the names of lodges: "Heavenly View," the "dinning room" (must be very loud in there), and "hole foods" (not meant to be religious).

I find the signs enchanting and inviting.

Almost as good as the "Beer, Wine and Plants"
sign near my home in Somerville, MA years ago.

I was unprepared, however, for the officiousness of a sign that read: "Do you have Climbing Permit?" Written in English on one side and Nepali on the other, the details were spelled out as follows:

- "It is illegal to climb any mountain peaks in Nepal without climbing permit.

- Nepal Mountaineering Association representatives and authorized local institutions or individuals may check your climbing permit, please co-operate them.

- Climbers involved in illegal climbing face prosecution as per the laws governing regulations of Nepal (Nepal Tourism Acts 2035 B.S. Article 3)

- Nepal Mountaineering Association does not recognize and certify successful ascent of illegal climbing.

- Nepal mountaineering Association does not certify individuals and accidents occurred during illegal climbing. Uncertified incidents and accidents may face legal complication to claim insurance.

- Only climber registered in the climbing permit are allowed to climb the mountain peak.

- Group leader and climbers are requested to make sure that a climbing permit is obtained to climb the desired peak.

- No one can profit from illegal climbing! So stop illegal climbing right now.

- Inform nearest police station in the event of death or disappearance of members of the team.

—CHOMRONG 2170 M Nepal Mountaineering association."

This came as quite a surprise, given the near absence of other regulations. I supposed it made sense; the authorities wanted no part of lawsuits from tourists who arrived unprepared and blamed the government for their troubles.

In any case, I couldn't remember seeing a police station here (not that I would even have recognized one). I was glad that someone else had taken care of the climbing permits and that we could just point to Lila if anyone questioned our paperwork.

My right arm was sunburned, a perfect example of how paying mindful attention to one thing can mean a complete lack of attention to another.

Breathing deeply, I slowly turned, taking in the depth of this valley tucked into a bowl of the Himalayas. We were on day four of our trek to the Annapurna Base Camp. There were no more vehicles to be seen, nor even donkeys or horses laden with provisions.

I felt relaxed and energized at the same time. The panorama continued to evolve, revealing frosted peaks even as we remained comfortable in pants and T-shirts. I had heard so many warnings about the cold and snow, but I hadn't thought about how warm it could be (probably in the high seventies and eighties at midday at this point, dropping into the forties or perhaps fifties at night). I had never considered how comfortable sandals or flip-flops might have been to wear off the trail.

The sun highlighted some tiny white flowers of early spring. We had not seen rain since the beginning of our trek, and the twigs and dried grass crackled in response to our quick but measured steps.

Lila was in the lead, carefully calibrating a steady but not exhausting pace. We were not hurried, as he had planned our daily walks with an eye toward arriving at each milestone on time. Amar, our porter, had long since passed this spectacular vista, his youthful strength speeding him ahead, even with the bulk of our belongings tied up with his own.

I began to hear a faint musical tune, which I didn't recognize until I sensed a pattern. My phone! Jwalant had given me a cell phone in Kathmandu in case we needed to get in touch. I raced to answer it.

"Hello?" I breathed.

Jwalant's distant voice asked, "Is that Meg or Kate?"

"It's Meg!" I shouted. The signal cut out abruptly. I called back, but the call cut out again. We repeated the same frustrating process. Shiiiit!

The splendor of being four days' walk from the road evaporated.

There was nothing I could do, but I felt queasy and unnerved. I knew Kate would solve any problems on her own before asking for help. Still, I was unaccustomed to being so completely unavailable to my family, and I struggled to calm myself.

I worked to keep my heart rate under control as we walked on. I was no longer noticing the stunning vista around me.

A few minutes later, the clear ringtone of Lila's phone pierced the air. After a moment, he handed it to me.

Jwalant's voice said, "Don't worry. Not a big problem. We just need a copy of the other side of Kate's student ID for her visa to Bhutan."

I blew out my breath. This was a minor stumbling block, not a tragedy.

That evening, I was able to secure a few minutes with a functioning computer, a task that required a hike from our lodge. It was worth the twenty-minute jaunt in each direction, even after seven hours of hiking.

"You sure jumped into Mama Bear mode," Lisa commented.

"Wouldn't you, if you thought your daughter was in some kind of trouble?" I countered.

Her voice was soft. "I'm not criticizing, just noticing."

Lisa is enjoying one of the many bridges we were able to cross.

I realized I was being defensive. Worry had been so far from my mind that it had caught me off guard.

I thought the call might leave me on edge, but in fact it renewed my confidence in my family and the resourcefulness of those around us. I relaxed again into the semi-meditative state that our trek inspired.

I realized that I could happily take my place in this universe—both vast and intimate enough to connect with those close to me—no matter the time and space between us.

A couple of days later, we were stopping for lunch ("Come us guest, leave us friend") when we noticed a group of young men. They had arrived just before us, and their guide was a Nepali man.

"How old do you think I am?" the men's guide asked us. "Twenty?" we ventured. (It turned out that Bishal was twenty-one.)

"I'm fifty-four, and Lisa is fifty-three," I blurted. I don't mind my age, never have, but it would have rankled if he had guessed that I was much older than Lisa.

"Where are you from?"

"The greater Boston area," I said, adding that I was originally from New York State.

"Oh, two brothers inside are from New York State," he responded. "Where in New York did you live?"

Outsiders often see New York State only as New York City and Everything Else, but it's home to many other cities both large and small, jagged mountains, and gorgeous rolling countryside.

"Well, my mom is now living in a little town called New Paltz, about ninety miles north of New York City."

"They're from New Paltz!" he exclaimed, gesturing toward the dining room. "Go in and talk to them!"

New Paltz is a town of seven thousand people, so the chances seemed remote that I would know them, even though travel is replete with unlikely "coincidences." The restaurant was perched on a ledge, with a sweeping vista on the other side. Bishal announced that Lisa and I were Americans and that I was from New Paltz.

Twenty-one-year-old Liam Purvis had a roundish, broad face and lively, dark eyes. He had been living in Korea, earning a living by kick-boxing. (Whaaaaat? I wondered how his mom felt about that.) Bosch, nineteen, was blonder with blue eyes, a bit taller, but with the same open demeanor and friendliness. Their father was connected to Bishal's father somehow, and they had already been in Nepal for a couple of weeks. Their companion was a Mexican named Ernesto, who had been on the road for several months, having started this trek on his own before running into them.

Climbers visit the Hudson Valley (and New Paltz in particular) from all over to practice rock climbing in the Shawangunk Mountains, known for steep expanses of rock and spectacular hiking. I made an immediate connection with the Purvis brothers, and we all felt an intangible connection with this spiritual locale.

We ran into them again the next evening at the lodge where we were all staying. The temperature had begun to drop, and at night it turned very cold. I was dressed in layers: two bottoms, three tops, part of my winter jacket, and two pairs of wool socks.

Lisa and I decided to purchase kerosene heat, which was delivered from underneath the table, so that we could actually feel our hands while we ate. (Through a gap in the floor, we could even see the worker turning on the heater below us.)

She and I agreed that the heat was well worth the price—at least until it became too smelly. But Lila was wary when we were asked to pay for the service the next day.

"Be very careful," he told us. "Don't let them take advantage of you. You cannot be cheated by these young men."

"It's OK, Lila. We're happy to pay." The extra charge amounted to less than ten dollars.

But Lila's smooth countenance was stern. "You be careful."

Liam had been traveling with his violin (his *violin?*), and after dinner I recorded him playing an Irish shanty. He was delighted with the instrument, having learned to play relatively recently. I, on the other hand, had refused to buy a bracelet, because I did not want to carry the extra weight!

I dubbed this the "Youth vs. Preparedness Tour." They had probably struck out on a lark: "Hey, let's climb to the Annapurna Base Camp! That'll be awesome!" Meanwhile, Lisa and I had been poring over lists of what and how much to bring. When I told the tour organizers that my sleeping bag was rated to fifteen degrees, they suggested I get a liner to ensure it was rated to zero. They were not fooling around. Jesus, *zero*? I was going to be sleeping in ZERO degrees?

But Bishal, Liam, and Bosch were clearly unencumbered with such detailed advice. They were clad in broken-in sneakers and little outerwear. It was already cold, and we still had another solid day's climb to get to the base camp. We offered up wool socks for them to use as mittens, and they accepted this small gift. We learned later that they had all been ill when starting their trek just a few days prior.

"We would have been fine if we stuck to Nepali food," Liam explained. "We had a Western meal prepared, and we all felt poorly afterward. My belly felt like a drum, it was so distended. Starting the climb, none of us could eat, and this was one of the most challenging things I have ever done." Coming from a kickboxer, that really meant something!

"The first couple of days were really rough," Bosch added, "but I learned that I could do this. It gave me confidence that I could take on bigger mountains."

I wondered whether their quick climb added to their initial discomfort. I was grateful that my own stomach upset had happened at the beginning of our hike, with the shortest climbing time. I can only imagine what it would have felt like to do six hours on a rumbly tummy.

Tres amigos: Liam, Bishal and Bosch. So fun to be able to share some of this journey with them. Violin not pictured here.

Liam recounted how he realized that his stomach was about to unburden itself. "We stopped to ask the local people if we could use their outhouse, which they obligingly pointed out. It was, of course, the hole-in-the-ground variety. My insides exploded—and there was nothing in the way of toilet paper to be found. We were back on our climb when we heard a shriek," he continued. "It was the woman whose outhouse I'd just defiled. 'Get back there and clean it up!' she hollered. 'How dare you leave it in such a state?' So I did the walk of shame back to the site and cleaned up as best as I could. It was absolutely mortifying."

I hadn't realized that we would be just meters away from Annapurna Base Camp for Leap Day, this delightful (and underrated) day. The concept of Leap Day has always captured my imagination. Its very name invites boldness. It's a time to try out new behaviors and ideas, a designated opportunity to bring freshness to life.

Julius Caesar (namesake of the Julian calendar) instituted the extra day to compensate for the extra quarter-day each year that differentiates the solar and calendar years. But because the actual difference is slightly less than a quarter-day—actually eleven minutes and fourteen seconds less—this minor discrepancy eventually threw the calendar off course by a full day.

Pope Gregory XIII (namesake of the Gregorian calendar) is credited with adjusting the formula to eliminate a leap year three times out of every four hundred years. A century year cannot be a leap year unless it is divisible by 400. So 1700, 1800, and 1900 were not leap years, but 1600, 2000, and 2400 all qualify.

I love that we have a day that pays homage to inexactness. And I increasingly value this concrete reminder that small increments can create big change. We cannot change the sun. We can only adjust our own behavior and accommodate our relationship to it. It feels good to stretch ourselves. Possibility lies within our capability. What better invitation than a day named for moving upward and forward? And what better place to celebrate it than the heart of the Himalayas, on a trip that forges relationships and extends my heart to the ones I already hold dear?

A few days into our trek, we stayed at Buddha Lodge, where we were treated to a hot shower and a bathroom that featured an actual toilet, with a seat and everything.

The lodge's valley location made me feel as if we were in a pocket, with the mountains surrounding us on every side. Our approach to the lodge had been a tad discouraging once we realized that we would have to descend in order to reach it—and then climb our way back out.

The atmosphere at the mostly vacant lodge was friendly. One of the few other guests was a woman whose youthful mother had turned sixty-five at the Annapurna Base Camp. A long-distance runner, she reminded us to get enough to eat while climbing. Although she knew it was critical to stay fueled, she had not eaten enough before the final ascent and found herself completely depleted of energy.

I tucked away that piece of advice: Eat snacks. Check.

That night, I lay awake, listening to gentle sleet on the tin roof: tat-tat-tat, pause, tat-a-tat-tat. TAT-TAT-TAT.

And then it started to come down in great torrents. TATAT TAT TATATAT TATATATATATTAT.

Lisa jolted upright in bed, a look of terror on her face, probably beset with visions of our little dwelling buried in snow.

"It's OK!" I shouted over the racket, trying to sound both calm and loud. "It's just hail!" She listened attentively for a moment and then visibly relaxed.

The cacophony continued for several minutes, reaching a rapid-fire crescendo. And then, as quickly as it started, it began to taper: TATATATA tatatatat. Tat-a-tat. Tat. We waited, holding our breath.

Lisa hopped out of bed and opened the door. "It's totally clear now!" she announced. "Let's go outside!"

I thought she was nuts but couldn't resist the opportunity to go out into the clear night. The stars were abundant and bright, as if polished by the passing shower. The quiet extended on and on, made more dramatic by the contrast with the mayhem we'd just endured. We stood in awe of our haven swaddled in a blanket of deep blue, its sparkles winking and scattered.

In the morning, as we began the day's ascent, we passed by nests of hailstones the size of robins' eggs.

Sometimes Lisa listened to her iPod, which she said she used as motivation (although, to my eyes, she never seemed to need any). I have always been sensitive to sound, and even the tinny sound that leaked from her earbuds was enough to distract me.

I adore music of all kinds, and it is a hugely important part of my life, but here in the Himalayas I needed complete immersion in my surroundings. I couldn't get enough of it: the slight gurgle of the brook hundreds of feet below, the rustle of the leaves, the crack of a branch. I was glad that Lisa did not take it personally when I decided to hang back from her.

Several days later, still on our way up to base camp, we passed through the avalanche field. The most likely time for avalanches is in the afternoon, when the sun hits the slopes and starts to melt them, Lila told us.

Although it was now early in the morning, he hurried us along, for the first and last time, his attitude all business.

We could easily see where the snow had created a wide swath that swept down the mountains in a vertical path, cutting into the landscape and creating its own valley. I tried not to think about the roar of sound it must have made as it came hurtling down, wiping out anything in its path. Even those who heard its approach could have been swallowed in the unforgiving deluge.

I felt my heartbeat quicken as I realized that my pace—between the altitude and the (admittedly small) pack I was carrying—was limited.

I shivered, and not from the cold. I wanted no part of lingering there and forced myself to think only of my steps and what lay in front of me. There was no room for anxiety.

In the ten minutes it took us to get across, I realized that nature could do some soberingly real and dramatic damage in swift order. It could do so without intent, prejudice, or preference, and it could not be persuaded or cajoled.

I appreciated that Lila was aware of the natural rhythm of these mountains, choosing carefully when we walked, and where. This mindfulness and acceptance of what is, this respect for the environment and the beings that inhabit it, made me grateful. The threat of avalanches had been a buzz of anxiety in the shadows, but Lila's care allowed us to live more completely in our surroundings.

Huge agricultural terraces dotted the landscape, like topographical

I cannot get enough of the steppes. They captivate me every time.

maps covered with moss or crops. They follow the shape of the land, dwarfing the humans and animals that call them home. The interplay between the life-sustaining crops and the people who tend them seemed a sacred bond.

I could not get enough of the stepped terraces. Some passages were much more closed and tight. I am mildly claustrophobic, and I felt more relaxed when I was able to see broader vistas, these gifts of light and panorama. The wide expanses of land were another reward for me.

At Machapuchare Base Camp, the last stop below Annapurna, we ran into the guys and shared a snack. They had been planning to head to Annapurna Base Camp the next day, but with the prediction of snow, they decided to start their ascent earlier.

It was bright and sunny, the sky an intense blue. As we began to climb, the temperature dropped abruptly, and the snow began to fly. The last couple of hours was marked by blinding, swirling snow. In preparation for the cold, we were wearing all our gear, but the completeness of the whiteout was the real challenge.

Once again, I placed my confidence in Lila. Up we traveled, my breathing increasingly labored. Occasional glimpses of a sign, or of the lodges themselves, confirmed that we were on course. Lisa was out of my sight line for the last hour.

On arriving at the lodge at Annapurna Base Camp, we unloaded our packs onto our beds. It was the first room we'd seen with multiple beds; it could clearly accommodate four or five easily. At least the path to the dining room was under roof cover, so we did not have to venture back into the raging storm to find it. The staff here slept on pads lining the dining room, unlike the other lodges, where their rooms were separate.

We ran into the quartet yet again. During the blizzard that raged, a tiny United Nations—representing Mexico, Nepal, Ireland, Germany,

Korea, Venezuela, Switzerland, Japan, and the United States—sat in the dining room, Gore-Tex jackets fully zipped. At a table that could seat twenty, a group played cards at one end while we at the opposite end decided to swap stories, providing entertainment for anyone who wanted to listen. Not surprisingly, all the stories were about travel, mishaps, and adventures.

I told the story of my cross-country trip in 1979, when I was twenty-two. I had been in San Francisco for three days when a stocky woman with long hair and heavy eye makeup demanded, "Aren't you going to say hello, Meg?"

I didn't know anyone there, except my old friend, Wild Bill, and I couldn't imagine how this unfamiliar woman could possibly know me.

Then she asked if I remembered Roger, the robust tenor who'd sung in various high school choruses with me. It turned out that this woman was Roger—en route to becoming Laurie.

In the middle of the night, all my excellent hydration necessitated a trip to the loo. Reluctantly, I layered up and slid the bolt back. The second I cracked the door, a small black dog slipped in and scurried underneath one of the beds. I remembered Lila's admonishment that we should not approach any of the animals, but I didn't have time to argue. When I returned to the room, Lisa drowsily agreed to leave the dog where he was for a few hours. There was no way we would put him out on such a bitter night, and he curled up with Lisa.

I learned later that Lisa and this dog had a history from the trip up to the base camp. Both Lisa and I had lived with dogs for many years and could not have been more delighted to share our space with this cunning sweetheart. But it would be many months before I learned how important a role he had played in her ascent to Annapurna.

Lisa had been eager to get to the base camp in the white-out blizzard, and this dog, who had been at the lower camp, led her there. Because Lisa suffered from massive headaches at the base camp (mine were alleviated by Tylenol), she started her descent in the morning, a little ahead of Lila and me. Feeling completely out of it, she was blindly making her way down the hill in waist-high snow, when this same small black dog arrived to guide her. He seemed to instinctively know that she needed his guidance. Trotting ahead, he helped turn what could have been a terrifying couple of hours into a direct path to shelter. She told me emphatically that she could not have made it without his assistance.

It turned out that, even earlier that morning, this dog had also guided the guys back to Machapuchare. The generosity of animals never ceases to delight, and I wondered how many people he had helped over the years. Perhaps he did so in hopes of small offerings, but he clearly seemed satisfied with a bed and human companionship. I thought warmly of my own brood back home: a rescue dog from Puerto Rico and two Maine coon cats and felt a bit homesick for these card-carrying members of our fam.

Lila insisted on an early-morning departure from base camp, and we hiked down to Bamboo, the only lodge we stayed at a second time. We made our way down cautiously but as quickly as possible in order to get to a more comfortable altitude. The farther we descended, the less snow there was. But with four feet of pristine snow cover, the path was still quite slippery.

We had lunch at Himalaya again before descending more. In the bright sunshine, the mountain views behind us were spectacular. The very tips of the mountains were backlit, and the wispy clouds surrounding them reminded me of early-morning mist rising from a chilly lake.

A little farther down, a dip in the terrain left some of the mountains in shadow, while just beyond, a series of snow-covered peaks stood in bright sunlight. The contrast was breathtaking.

The majesty of these mountains exceeds the capability of my lens.

Just a few steps more, the rock was tilted, its striations layered as if with powdered sugar. Each layer pointed inward, and right in the center of the V, the sun was rising, bright white at the bottom, fading to light blue and finally azure at its broadest point. Closer to us, gray rocks appeared from the snow-covered, jagged peaks set back behind trees encased in shadow.

I could feel Lila trying to be patient as we stopped to photograph and absorb our surroundings. (Lisa had slipped and hurt her ankle on the way down, which made for another complication.) This was a longer hike, and so his timetable was a bit stricter. But this was what we had come here to see—all of it. We were looking at the top of the world, and we knew that we would not be back anytime soon. We had to let it settle into our bones. I wanted to take the feeling home with me.

It had started to rain a bit before we got to our lodge, and minutes before we arrived, it started to pour. As I adjusted my poncho to cover both my body and my pack, I realized that we had been lucky with the weather. It was very cold here, unlike the mildness of a few days earlier. It was of course not the cold of Annapurna Base Camp, but I still needed to wear three layers.

Farther down we passed a man carrying huge bushel baskets of leaves hanging from a bamboo pole slung over one shoulder. His dark brown skin, black hair, and mustache coordinated with his black pants, white shirt, plastic sandals, and pale red cap. I couldn't fathom even one day of lugging anything up and down the steep mountainside. But it was just another day's work for him, intensely physical and necessary for survival.

I thought about how everyone's experience of this landscape is uniquely their own. Even one day would change what you saw, who you met, how you felt. The trail to Annapurna Base Camp would be awash in thousands of huge magenta rhododendrons—a favorite of mine—in just a few weeks. The storm had covered the trail in slick snow, covering what flowers had already emerged. There were no monkeys to be seen. It was clear and bitter cold the following morning, likely portending a beautiful day ahead. No hailstorm this time. Yet, two days earlier we had arrived in shirtsleeves.

If we had planned our trip later in the season, we might have had to deal with leeches, which, when the river is higher, are said to be unavoidable. My stomach lurches at the very idea of these creepy bloodsucking hitchhikers. Would I have preferred them to the threat of avalanches? Could have been a dealbreaker.

Lila promised a completely different view of the mountains from the village of Potaka, farther down, where we would overnight before arriving in Pothana and our flight back to Kathmandu. I had thought little of what would come next, having focused on ascending to the base camp.

I had read the Lama Yeshe book of teachings, and this connected me to Kate and what she was studying. Being a visual person, I was grateful for the imagination to picture her at Kopan and to send my thoughts there.

As the teachings suggest, I tried to maintain an open mind and open heart and not feel an attachment to things. That was something to aspire to. Maybe that was the trick: to enjoy material things if I have them, but not to be upset if I lose them—or never acquire them.

I realized how much I needed the space, the movement, and the time to drink in the deep beauty of these magnificent mountains. No wonder people are spiritual here. It is impossible to live in such a place and deny the existence of something greater than oneself. The mountains shape everything: what people do, how they think, what they find possible. The mountains unite, but they also divide, in terms of making travel so arduous. The landscape preserves a way of life, even as the tourism it spawns, ironically, challenges it.

KATE: *Journal excerpt, 2/28,* 5:30 a.m.: I would have liked to do some journaling last night and earlier today, but I now have a room-mate, who is from Sacramento. This change seems to be a message about cleanliness in my life. I can no longer use the other bed as a temporary place to put things. I have to be more mindful of where I leave my books, etc. Ah well, you learn to accept, right?

The first teaching yesterday was about dissatisfaction, which connected strongly to my learning about happiness so far. The concept of creating our own reality is almost identical with Elizabeth Gilbert's description of how the mind paints a picture, instead of taking a photograph.

The points on virtuous action connect to Aristotle as well. I've picked up that an important constant throughout happiness definitions is intelligence. Human beings are intelligent. And human beings (like all sentient beings) strive for happiness. But because we have this intelligence, humans won't be happy just sitting around the way dogs do. And that is why cultivation of the mind will make us happy, as it is also what makes us intelligent.

Aristotle completely supports this. Gilbert essentially supports this, saying we can live in the present and trust others. Gretchen Rubin supports this concept as well, in her point of challenge and mastery. So that first teaching was great, giving me a lot to think about (although it was extremely painful to sit on the floor for that long).

Then we broke into discussion groups and talked a lot about contentment versus happiness. I made the point that it's not enough to be content, that happiness is the real goal. The person we looked to for the most Buddhist knowledge disagreed, saying that with age, one finds that contentment is enough. And we had a whole conversation on it.

I felt a little uneasy, being so young, which I hadn't felt here before. It wasn't that I didn't have anything to say, it was that I did, and others didn't. Nothing to really worry about, just being shy.

The last teaching and meditation were centered around karma. This interests me but forces me to suspend my disbelief about past lives (probably bad karma to say that). Not impossible by any means, but the teachings just don't connect with me as naturally. And people are very interested! Maybe I will find a deeper way to connect with it today.

I am quite enjoying my time here, even with the hard mental work (and physical discomfort!). The silent morning begins.

KATE: *Journal excerpt, 2/29, 5:35 a.m.:* I do this journal entry five minutes later each morning! I need to stop the trend. Waking up early still isn't too hard, but I'm tired and I just wander around. Who knew sitting on a cushion for more than eight hours a day could make me feel so exhausted and sore?

Yesterday we had more teachings on karma, followed by discussion on the topic, all of which I was having a very hard time with. It's the biggest reminder that Buddhism is a religion. You have to believe in karma, or else you won't be happy. And you'll actually be creating negative karma. And a purification process requires at least a small ritual.

Whether I believe in karma is irrelevant to me right now. Sure, for this week I absolutely believe, so I can get a fuller experience, but I just don't know after that. How could it be that a person who's done non-virtuous things—gathered complete negative karmic actions—can't get rid of their negative karma if they start to turn their life around by doing positive actions, just because they're not Buddhist and don't know the purification process?

To me, this looks like forcing a religion onto people. Sure, they tell you that if you don't believe in karma that's fine, you'll just come back

to it later, when you have the mental capacity to understand. And the
kicker is that it's just your karma if you don't understand.

On the other hand, the afternoon teaching was about attachment,
and I could very closely identify with that! It doesn't tell you to give up
all attachments or pleasures. Just be aware of them so that you don't end
up causing yourself suffering.

The meditation on this was really great. I could focus better than I
had been able to before, and I feel my thinking was productive. I learned
things about myself that I didn't know. I hope to keep this energy going
(and figure out a better way to sit).

Our evening session was a showing of *The Unmistaken Child*,
a movie about a reincarnated lama. It was pretty crazy, and I'm still
unsure of how I feel about it.

The child in the movie lives here, though, and is now about eight
years old. We will meet him on Saturday!

KATE: *Journal excerpt, 2/29, 8:17 a.m.:* Focus meditation is much,
much harder than analytical meditation. This is where I struggle most
in the day. But today was not so bad. I am good at maintaining focus
after the meditation—when I am walking, eating, and now lying in the
sun, for example. I just need to figure out how to bring that focus into
the actual meditation.

I really cherish the silent mornings. I don't think I would have a
problem doing the rest of the day in silence as well, but right now I feel
no need to be in full silence.

I've started to think about the comparison of my happiness here
to my happiness at home. Overall, I think they are about equal. Right

now I am completely overjoyed at my location, my practice, and the people I'm meeting. But I don't think that my happiness at home seems smaller, worse, or less "real."

I have noticed that the components of Buddhism I identify with are already part of my life. I exercise a large amount of acceptance and as much compassion as I can in my daily life. I will definitely try to bring home more time for silence and solitary reflection, even if it isn't always in the form of meditation. I will also try to be more conscious of the food I eat and take the time to make my bed.

MEG: I've noticed the incessant jangling of donkeys here, trotting tirelessly up and down the stairs and hills. They gotta be some muscly critters, bedecked with blankets and bells that make them seem festive (except that they do not exhibit any sense of the festivity). They take their work seriously and need to watch their steps. One misstep could be costly and painful. I can almost hear them mumbling, "Don't these people ever get tired of slogging up and down these hills? Do they really need all this oil/food/paper/whatever other supplies?" But this is their life, and people depend on them.

It is a kind of relationship that is unfamiliar to me. We have always had dogs and cats as pets, but I have never lived on a farm or been around working animals. I know that sheepherding dogs love to work. When Kate and I visited a farm in Ireland, the numerous dogs all seemed eager to bring in the sheep. Their DNA propels them to yearn to work in a big way.

We passed water buffalo on the trail now and then. Sometimes they stood just off the path, eyeing us calmly, sometimes on a farm, but they felt quintessentially of the region. Some of my favorite photos show their broad visages and spectacularly long horns. They would make most excellent drying racks for laundry.

Could not be more delighted to share the path with these photogenic animals.

The name Jhinu Hot Springs was spelled out in huge letters on the roofs of its buildings, as if to mark it for guests arriving by air, although I did not spot a helipad or airport. The village of Jhinu, a collection of hotels and hostels, was almost European looking, with flower boxes hanging from many of the windows.

Tired as we were after six hours of hiking (albeit mostly downhill), even in the pouring rain, we absolutely needed to trek the extra half hour to the natural hot springs.

I had not prepared for this little delight, and in lieu of a bathing suit, I borrowed a camisole from Lisa. The springs were divided into men's and women's areas, although for some reason a large Korean man was holding forth in the women's area.

I heard myself suggesting that we all sing "You Are My Sunshine." Don't ask me where that came from, but the Korean contingent burst out in unison. It turned out that they knew more of the lyrics than the English speakers did! Music is such a terrific unifier. The song uplifted us, transcending the rain and the hours of hiking. It reminded me how connected we are, on so many levels, across the globe.

I found it a bit disconcerting to find that there were many more guests staying here than at the other lodges. A large, rather deaf Englishwoman at a nearby table sounded like Julia Child, her strident voice carrying over the entire space. Although comical, it also felt like an intrusion.

We were served our hot lemon tea in Tweetie mugs, reminding us that we were much closer here to Western influences. The day before, we ordered ginger tea, now a favorite, which arrived in rooster mugs. Lisa asked our waiter where the ginger was. He walked away, returned, and threw some chopped ginger into our mugs with one dirty hand. Careful what you wish for, indeed.

KATE: *Journal excerpt, 2/29, 9:30 p.m.:* Losing what we want can lead to anger, a mental state.

Anger is produced by attachment; it amplifies bad qualities.

Aversion: I don't want _____. I want to be separate.

Anger: I'm mad at _____.

Hatred: Intensified anger

It is OK to show "ruffledness" as long as it is in the right motivation.

Anger is directed at an object (mostly a person). It is due to harm directed in our direction (generally) or an expectation not being met (someone cutting in line; we feel victimized and that it's "unfair").

Understanding the terrible things that happen through karma lowers the agitation but doesn't condone it or mean you shouldn't try to do anything about it.

The basic antidote is patience. It's not that we don't respond, as long as the mind is calm. What is the motivation? Patience is the armor of the mind.

Anger is punishing yourself for someone else's mistake. Forgiveness is important, a sign of positive self-esteem.

KATE: *Journal excerpt, 2/29, 3:30 p.m.:* Teachings: Ignorance is the cause of attachment and anger. It is not stupid but bound by suffering. There are three types of ignorance: the ignorance of (not believing in) karma, the ignorance of rebirth, and the ignorance in belief of "I."

"I" is a hallucination. It's a fundamental ignorance. If there is an "I," there is a "my." This leads to attachment and negative reaction. This blocks compassion. Personality and identity exist, but not in the way we think. Where is the person? Body, mind, and identity don't make up the "I" (which is the conventional definition of "I").

KATE: *Journal excerpt, 3/30:* I accidentally slept until 5:40 this morning, no time to journal.

Yesterday was good! The morning teaching was about anger, and it was not very difficult to understand. It made a lot of sense to me and was again something I could identify with. He described "angry" as the opposite of "happy," which I really like. And as Venerable Palzang said, "No one looks pretty or handsome when they're mad."

An important lama came around 2 in the afternoon, and we were allowed into the main *gompa* (structure or building for religious learning or study) to see the welcoming ceremony.

It was incredible. As he arrived, everyone lined up to offer him *khatas* (silk scarves) as a sign of respect. Inside the *gompa* were only high monks and Westerners (which was a little weird). There was a lot of chanting, more chats, and then tea with small candies or cookies. We saw the young reincarnate from last night's movie. This typical Tibetan welcoming ceremony for someone of his level of respect was beautiful.

Afterward, we went to the afternoon teaching about the third afflictive emotion of ignorance. This was very confusing, another hard one to grasp. The first two parts were about not believing in karma and reincarnation. I just kind of let that be. The last part is the ignorance of believing in "I" in the conventional sense. I have heard this philosophy before; it takes a while to wrap my mind around it.

The last teaching of the day was from another confirmed reincarnated lama. He is nineteen years old and studies at another monastery, in India. He is at university there and has been for *six years*—with another fourteen to go! It was great to hear him speak. He's not arrogant, but rather very open and frank. He says he doesn't remember his past life and that it doesn't make him learn much faster than his peers. He's just more easygoing than they are.

He talked about how monks are regular people (he likes to listen to Eminem!), and that when he's feeling stressed sometimes, he'll just talk to a friend. But then he also talked about acceptance being what touches his heart the most, and how the Supreme Emotions (love and compassion) are the most important things. He also said that sometimes he doubts some Buddhist teachings, and that we should keep questioning everything.

He made Buddhism very real and modern and accessible again. He talked like a regular teenager (lots of "so's" and "yeah's"), but he had such wisdom. Smiling the whole two hours he was talking.

Meditation was difficult this morning, but easier than last night. Turns out meditating on anger and attachment can make my mind agitated! Breathing is easy compared to that.

MEG: We crossed so many bridges over the course of our hike, over crevasses large and small, deep ravines, and shallow rivers, each one connecting the wild, sometimes inhabited mountains. Lush greenery on either side invariably made a lovely sight. Sometimes the bridge was built close to the ground, covering a wide expanse of river.

The bridges themselves were often swaying, sometimes crude-looking structures, but I knew that they had carried many people before me, and I loved the adventure of walking across. I also loved how they yielded to our steps. Sometimes it was best if we paced ourselves going across, in order to keep the weight consistent and not overtax it.

Each bridge was a reminder to take a breath, to notice the connections created to trade with, take care of, and travel to one another. Even at their most basic, each one had its own beauty. We could not have made this trip without them.

The bridges reminded me that I was in Nepal, and not somewhere closer to home. I was drawn to the unfamiliarity, comforted by it, even. The bridges were in tune with the mountains themselves. The materials were natural (rope and wood), and they were uneven. While I appreciate the efficiency and dependability of Western structures, I loved the blending of the bridges with this environment.

I was forced to trust that they were safe enough for our passage. I wondered how they were monitored for defects. Were they regulated by a governmental body? Who was responsible for repairs? I loved that the answers to these questions were not obvious, and I suspended any notion of officiousness in the name of adventure and travel.

Of course, it was still important to know when to be cautious and when to avoid a dangerous situation, no matter how inconvenient or irritating it might be.

But it was freeing to put my faith out there, allowing the moment to take over, nudging out any questions or doubts. It was a way to live fully right then, breathing in the pristine, cool air and drinking in the beauty of the shapes the mountains created and evolved, each view different from the last.

In just a few short months, both Gale and Kate would be out of the house, and this was a bridge of a different sort. I needed to find some way to prepare for life with a new focus, a way to spend my time that would feel satisfying and fulfilling.

Being a social worker in private practice was very important to me, and this was the first time that I had been away for more than a week in the nearly twenty-five years that I had been practicing. This was part of the way in which I needed to take care of myself, and it was important

These bridges are the funnest. You can't help but be fully present.

for my clients to know that I was doing so. A very capable colleague was covering for me, and I had total conviction that she could help anyone who needed it. There might be challenges, but each one had the capabilities to sort things out, or to find the people to help with the sorting.

This required a kind of trust—just as I came to feel about the safety of the bridges—to believe that everyone would be fine in my absence. It was a tricky balance to acknowledge my own importance without overstating it. I had worked hard to establish a trusting and productive relationship with my clients, and part of that involved allowing for time to do what is important to me. They are well able to understand this, even if my absence at a particularly inconvenient time might cause some anger.

I was so engrossed in where I was, what we were doing, and who was around us that it almost felt disrespectful to divert attention from the mountains, the trek, the now. Still, I wondered again how Kate was doing. And I loved the recent email message I had received from Duke. My mom had called him, though, which was a little nerve-wracking.

I didn't know when I would get back to internet communication. Not tonight. Maybe tomorrow, but doubtful. Certainly in Pokhara, which was three days away.

I realized how accustomed I had become to being in touch whenever it felt convenient. The immediacy of digital connectedness made me realize how different life felt without it.

Weddings here are scheduled for what are deemed to be auspicious days, and so they are often held during the week, not at what we Westerners might consider convenient weekend times. I loved the purity of this decision, although as a planner it would make me berserk to organize one. Or maybe not! If I too regarded chosen days as a clear priority in wedding planning, I suppose everything would just flow from there.

We walked from 7:45 a.m. to 3:45 p.m., with about an hour's break. That's 2,100 meters, which is to say a long way. On the climb back up to Chommrong, a sign announced the distance to be two thousand steps. After what seemed like forever, I asked Lila if we had done one thousand. No, he said, there were still around 1,800 to go. My heart sank. Quantifying is not helpful. It is better for me to just know that it's a bunch.

This whole trek has been like stepping back in time, centuries worth. It is astounding to see how much walking the people here regularly do—and with food, chickens, whatever on their backs.

I was stunned at the loads that people could carry either on their backs, or with a band strapped around their heads.

We reached Bichuk Deurali around 3. It is a lovely little town. Can't believe tonight is the last night. Tomorrow is just a couple of hours' trek.

Pothana, the town where we are spending our final night in the mountains, is the most personal and quaint place yet, my favorite so far.

We continue to see people we had met along the trek. Sarah and Sayaka, girls we had met at the Annapurna Base Camp, were the only other visitors staying in this little village, but in a different hotel. We stayed at See You Lodge and Restaurant. So sweet and welcoming, with a wood stove and music playing. The kitchen is accessible, clean, and filled with innumerable hanging pots and pans of every size. The owner said that he had trained in a five-star restaurant in India. And now he was here, in the middle of nowhere, days' walk from anywhere, waiting for tourists to come through. Did he not need any more stimulation? Relationships? Conversation? How did he keep things going? Did the food come to him? Did he ever need to leave here? He spreads his joy by staying still, and having people come to him. It is evidently enough.

Lisa and I had a beer, our first on this trip, which was great fun. We hadn't wanted to tax our brains while ascending, especially if it might have amplified our response to the altitude. And this is the first time that I've truly felt too warm at night. Down to only two layers, with one coming off very soon.

On the way down to Pokhara, we saw another school. I noticed slogans posted above the doorways: "Thinking well is wise. Planning well is wiser. Doing well is wisest." A little farther we passed by a woman who spread out yucca to dry in the sun. It lay in front of her on a blanket, and she sat tending to it as if to a young child.

At the end of the trail, we were picked up and transported back to Pokhara. Lila was so kind to point out that I was the largest of the four of us (at five foot five and 135 pounds), and so merited the front seat.

Drying yucca on the side of the path.

(Lisa later mentioned that when she was sitting next to Amar, our porter, he had made sure that no body parts, including their knees, touched
at any point.) I was worried that riding in front would be frightening,
but, even though the streets were busy and crowded, drivers were not
aggressive or super fast. This hardly compared to the density and intensity of Kathmandu.

Along the way, we saw a procession of a highly regarded lama (who
we thought might actually have been the Dalai Lama) in a car decked
out in flowers.

It was a bit of a culture shock to arrive back here in the city, where there
was so much to take in. There are more dwellings here, grouped closer

together. Some have thatched roofs and are surrounded by terraces and fields in shades of brown and tan.

Lisa and I separated during the afternoon to shop. I left my iPad to charge, but when we returned, I discovered that there was no electricity from 2 p.m. to 7 p.m. Then on until 10 p.m., and off until 5 a.m. the next day. Then on again until 2 p.m., and then off until 7. Interesting system, and one that I can only assume makes sense for them. My relationship to internet access is becoming more obvious. I had hoped to head off an avalanche of emails on my return.

We both shopped up a storm on our last night together. Lisa is a shopping pro. She even bought me an elephant-patterned skirt that I wore to dinner with my clunky walking shoes. No matter: It was a treat just to be in something clean.

I'm sure we're both ready for some time away from each other, but I'm sad too. We've done really well traveling together. I have gained such respect for this lively, creative woman and her innovative approach to her profession.

We ate at a restaurant called Boomerang, recommended by a contact Lisa had made on the flight over. It featured "Nepali culture," which included music and dancing and a good meal of vegetable curry and naan, strawberry ice cream on apple cake for dessert, and a small bouquet of flowers from the waiter. The owner, a "big man on campus" sort of person, was friendly, well meaning, and cheery. It felt like he was expecting something, but it was not clear what. Referrals? A big tip?

We watched a dozen paragliders on Pokhara's big, glassy lake. The town itself is sweet. With lots of trekking supplies and guides, the place felt like it could be in Tuscany as easily as the foothills of the Himalayas. One endearing sign near the soft pashmina scarves read as follows:

An irresistible request.

I tried to readjust to city noises after all the roosters and goats and stars. I love the cities but end up yearning for the sounds of the crickets and countryside after a short time. These different realms of sound form a complementary yin and yang, both a part of our world.

We ran into Bishal, who, like us, is going back to Kathmandu. Maybe we would be able to get together there.

Mostly, though, I was excited to see Kate the next day. There was no way to let her know when I would be arriving, highlighting again how unaccustomed I was to this kind of loose communication. Pinpointing meeting times via texting feels easy and efficient by comparison.

I did get some shut-eye, but it was minimal. The beds were the hardest we had encountered, there was a persistent smell of methane, and some guy was coughing and spitting up a storm—so gross—at 5 a.m. At 6 we were pleased to discover that we had electricity, but after about ten minutes, it faded to black. No luxuriating in a long, hot shower, but there was enough warm water for a quick wash.

At Pokhara airport, Lisa and I awaited our Buddha Air flight back to Kathmandu. Boarding anytime now. Precision was not the name of the game in Nepal. Time was a generality, an approximation, a roundabout version of what is possible or needed. But things seemed to get accomplished as necessary.

A wedding party was also waiting in the terminal.

The groom looked radiant and spiffy, as did his (I assume) father. The groom's suit was black, with a bright-red shirt and thin black tie. Around his neck and shoulders, he wore a strikingly beautiful grass shawl with multicolored beads woven into it. The father was in a gray pinstripe suit, white shirt, red sweater, and red tie. Their fez-like hats were of a pink/green/yellow print. I wondered what the wedding would be like, where it would be, how the bride was doing. The groom's eyes were positively glowing; he was ready for this next step.

KATE: *Journal excerpt, 3/2, 8:23 p.m.*: I've decided to abandon my early-morning journal entry. I'm completely exhausted by the time I get to bed at 10:30. Tea is at 6 a.m., and we're not done until 9:30-ish at night. Who knew sitting could be so tiring?

Yesterday's discussion was really good. We talked about selflessness for about half an hour. I don't understand it in my heart, but I have a pretty good understanding in my head (I'm not sure if it's my brain or mind).

Then we saw the relics, which was absolutely fascinating. Relics are small pearls or stones or bones that come from the cremated body of a highly enlightened being. They are in the lama's retreat room (he was basically the head lama of Kopan), which was filled with figures and *khatas* and lights. The relics were in little glass bowls in a container that looked like a fish tank. They are so holy that one gets purified in terms of karma simply by looking at them. Then, with traditional Tibetan hospitality, the monk showing us the relics offered us candy on our way out. I'm still not sure what to make of it.

The 3:30 teachings started to get into the concept of emptiness, which is insane. Basically everything comes from Dependent Arising, meaning everything depends on something else to come into existence, so everything is empty. I don't understand the connection yet.

At 5:45 p.m. we meditated on "I" and "emptiness." It was a good meditation, in the sense that my focus was there, but I feel as though I wasn't thinking in the desired way. We were told to look for "I" in different parts of ourselves, but I thought it was useless, because my belief is that "I" is made up of all parts of ourselves.

Then we were told to locate the mind, but again the point was lost on me. I kept coming back to *Stumbling on Happiness*, the Daniel Gilbert book. A patient with frontal lobe damage couldn't say what he was doing tomorrow, because that would require planning, and that part of his brain was damaged. When asked what it was like to think about "tomorrow," he replied that it felt like being asked to find a chair in an empty room. It just wasn't there.

His brain didn't have the capacity to conceptualize "tomorrow," just like our brains can't conceptualize things like "infinity." I feel like conceptualizing the mind is just the same as "infinity." We're looking for a chair in an empty room.

The 7:45 p.m. activity was supposed to be a light offering, but instead ended up being a two-hour-long explanation of taking refuge (which is something like a Buddhist baptism). At the end we were asked how many people were planning on taking refuge, and the answer was around ten people, out of ninety. It was an interesting but very, very long explanation of something that had little, if any, relevance to me.

This morning's tea and the sunrise were as wonderful as ever. Morning meditation was good. We started with a meditation that required breathing in with one nostril and out of the other, imagining energy flow and things like that. I felt like a crazy person, but it actually worked for me. Focusing on the rest was difficult, but not awful. I'm enjoying it more and more, I think. Time to bask in the sun and read dharma.

KATE: *Journal excerpt, 3/2:* Time is the moment after another. Present is dependent on the past. Future is dependent on the present, dependent arising.

The mind labels the combination of body and mind as "I." The label is the only thing that exists. Conventionally there is an "I," but there's no "I" relation between dependent arising and emptiness. The concept of "I" depends on life history, and there's no "I" that doesn't depend on something else. "I" is a feeling that creates "mine." If something is "mine," it can't be "yours." It is a false sense of separation between "mine" and "yours."

A clock comes about because of causes and conditions. It is dependent. Because it is dependent, it doesn't exist on its own, and it is empty of inherent existence. Because everything is dependent, everything is inherent emptiness. Emptiness equals empty of inherent existence but does not equal nonexistent.

Realization of emptiness is seeing a clock and not perceiving it as a clock. Seeing everything, direct perception of emptiness, is surreal. It isn't real but still functions. Liberation from existence, emptiness and liberation from attachment. You realize nothing really functions. There's no badness when everything is dependent arising, causes and conditions, and karma.

(Why does the knowledge of attachment, impermanence, emptiness, etc., make loss or terrible acts OK? Some of the concepts are elusive and difficult to grasp.)

Five aggregates make up our body and mind: form, feelings, mental composition, discrimination, and mental consciousness. There is an "I" that exists based on this. It functions and makes choices and has free will; it just doesn't exist independently. Karma can function because it is dependent arising.

Neutrality is the goal. With the understanding of emptiness comes acceptance. Is neutrality really happy? It's not a feeling. The level of the mind is always a little bit happy, content at a higher level. Why are monks so happy? Suffering is a sensation; happiness is just a lack of suffering. Buddhas can teach others to take away suffering, and that is the benefit to all sentient beings of becoming enlightened.

KATE: *Journal reflections:* Today is the last day of the course! Just one session left. The most productive part of my day yesterday was with a couple of people who were in my discussion group. It helped me come to a lot of big points about happiness and my time here.

I want to start off with a couple of things. First, I am not a religious person. I never have been. It's always made me a little uncomfortable. But I have absolute respect for religion and anyone who chooses to practice it. Second, I have been having an incredible time at Kopan. It's beautiful, the people are fascinating, and I have learned so, so much.

That being said, I'm feeling very frustrated. More and more of what I learn about Buddhism seems to turn it into a self-perpetuating trap. The Buddhist path to enlightenment is the *only* way to be truly happy. To get to the point of being able to reach enlightenment, one has to have good enough karma to be introduced to dharma. To have good enough karma, one has to purify negative karma and gain positive karma. The easiest way to do this is to chant mantras, pray, give offerings (money) to Buddha, and walk around the stupa. Again, if this isn't making sense, it's because your karma isn't good enough. Maybe next lifetime.

And finally, the enlightened mind you're aiming for, everlasting happiness, is a content mind: one that still feels things but is not bothered by that. And the way that enlightened, omniscient mind will help all sentient beings is by teaching dharma. Which most of us have too much negative karma to understand anyway.

KATE: *Journal reflections:* I realized that I'm not sure if I want a perfectly even mind. This week is a pretty good look at what contentment means. I'm above neutral, with definitely positive feelings. No euphoria, no deep sadness. I really, really like it, especially for this period of time, but I don't think it could sustain me forever.

I have never subscribed to the philosophy of needing ups and downs to have the ups be really worthwhile, but now I am leaning more in that direction. It leaves room to grow and be human. Maybe I'm just thinking this because I've had the good fortune for my lows to not be too low. For someone whose ups and downs bring an overall negative feeling, maybe being consistently above neutral is the better option. But it's all perspective.

I want to use Buddhism to make my lows less low, but not to make my highs less high. I try to live passionately, and it seems difficult to do that when I'm trying to subdue my mind. Buddhism tries to drive home the point that there is no inherently existing "I," and I believe that's true. So why am I supposed to strip down the causes and conditions (my likes, dislikes, attachments, angers) that make me who I am? What am I left with?

Can't I define what happiness is for myself? With some exceptions, isn't a person's happiness true if she feels it? Buddhism would say no, that it's a delusion created by the mind. Sure! We create our own realities, yes, but that's what they become: realities!

It's hard for me to accept (karma) that there is only one path to happiness, as laid out by one being. It feels very limiting. The only way to reach true happiness is dharma, which you're encouraged to check out and question, but ultimately it is the only truth. That just raises more and more problems for me.

I'm afraid I'm sounding ranty, so I'll wrap it up. From Buddhism, I'll try to take home a less attached and calmer mind. I will act with compassion and a virtuous motivation. But I'll also take home some travel experience and the desire to travel more. I'll take home memories of the landscape and the interesting people from all over the world.

I've learned so much. I'm curious to see what the next few days at Kopan will bring—and the next leg of my journey with my mom!

KATE: *Journal excerpt,* 3/5, 10:25: Not much is happening in the way of Buddhism now, but I'm having a great time. I went into Boudha yesterday, walked around, and had dinner there. Around thirty people from the monastery showed up.

As people start to leave, I can't help thinking about impermanence and attachment. I've had great times with so many different people here. Some I may see again, some I may speak to, and some may be out of my life forever. But it's not sad, because the time we had together was still valuable, and an impact was made. I'm glad to have met them.

Now I'm just hanging around with the people who are left, enjoying the sun and one another's company. There are so many nuns and monks here at a prayer festival, all praying and singing. The head monk was throat singing for about forty minutes; it was totally insane.

My mom comes sometime tomorrow, and then we head back to Kathmandu on Wednesday. I look forward to seeing her. I may head back into Boudha soon. Walking is the greatest goodness of all!

KATE: *Journal excerpt,* 3/6, 9:37 a.m.: I am journaling to the sound of Tibetan throat singing, and the head monk speaking in Tibetan.

The prayer festival is still going on, including a debate in the Tibetan style. The monks all gather around, with the high monks (who basically have PhDs in Buddhism and who can be identified by yellow hats that resemble mohawks) sitting on the stage and facing the crowd. Students approach and ask them questions. But there are so many views within

Buddhism that the students ask questions about opposing points. They push each other out of the way to get to the microphone, always clapping their hands (which means, I'm pretty sure, emphasizing that they agree). When they slap the back of one hand on top of the other palm, that means "Shameful, you're wrong!" It's all very cool to watch.

I went into Kathmandu yesterday. I'm basically out of money, but even walking around is fun. We went to Durbar Square, which has lots of Hindu temples made of wood and brick. They're all so old, but well preserved.

By the time I got back to Kopan, it was nighttime. All the gompas were draped in lights for the prayer festival. I'm really glad that I'm here to see it looking so beautiful.

I did a light offering with a couple other people. It was definitely ritualistic, but still nice. Even though it is an offering, it still felt like it was beneficial to me. Who knows? Maybe I will come around to Buddhism sometime.

MEG: Although I was eager to get up to Kopan, and Kate, upon our return to Kathmandu, Lisa and I made time for lunch with Jwalant at a lovely place in Kamel. We wound our way through the labyrinth of the city and then found ourselves in an outdoor courtyard, the only patrons of a melon-colored, washed-stucco building. Tasty Thai food, so fresh. In some ways, Lisa and I had known a lot about each other, particularly with regard to work issues, but in other ways, we had started this adventure as complete strangers. Together, we had hiked for days, gloried in the most stunning scenery I could imagine, worried about avalanches, deciphered words from our guide, hesitated over the ginger thrown into our tea by a grubby-handed waiter, and wandered the streets in cities thousands of miles from home. We discussed our families and our histories. We had seen each other feel unwell, and we had seen each other burble with excitement over a waterfall.

With a big hug and a wave, I watched Lisa stride away in the long skirt she had purchased in Pokhara. In a moment, she blended in with the stream of people buzzing through Kathmandu. She looked purposeful and confident. I was sad to part from her, but at the same time I was eager to see Kate.

It was three o'clock by the time I reached the monastery. I was antsy to see Kate, but I knew that impatience would get me nowhere. Besides, I had complete trust that all would be as it needed to be.

I did wonder, however, how she would feel about my arrival. She had been on her own, doing this thing by herself. Would she be ready for me to shift how she had been living for the past twelve days? Maybe even eager to get away?

After winding his way around the potholes and up the steep hill, my driver dropped me off at the front gate. The man at reception gave me general directions to Kate's room, "near the stupa," which I hoped would become obvious as I got closer (lest I look stupid). I walked past cream-colored walls with brick-red trim, found the right door number, and turned the key.

"Hey!" Kate looked tanned and relaxed. She was wearing a pair of harem pants, which she must have picked up here, and a printed scarf. She was chatty, ready to talk about the people she had met, her experiences, and the place itself. It was a delight to see her, and I felt relief flood through me. The first minutes told me Kate was well: smiling, calm, and welcoming.

I was immediately taken back to her very first time away from home for more than a night. She had spent a week at Rowe Camp and Conference Center, in the western part of Massachusetts. As we strode up the road and around the bend leading to the camp dining room, the trees a canopy of light green, I saw Kate's beaming nine-year-old face. Her long, curly blonde hair was in a loose braid, and wisps framed her face in a soft, unruly halo. When she spotted us, she skipped down to meet us, and her smile expanded across her suntanned face. I had never seen her quite so freewheeling and relaxed (after just *one week!*). She was eager to have us meet her new friends and tell us what they had been doing. Her newfound confidence was like a cloak that billowed out behind her as she hopped over branches and stones. It was as if she had walked these paths all her life.

Here in Kopan was the seventeen-year-old version. Kate had clearly immersed herself in the program and in twelve days had made it her own. She had evidently become comfortable in this place and considered herself a part of the group. She had embraced the people, the teachings (to a point, anyway), and the country itself. She was happy to take the lead in exploring and showing me around.

I loved this new version of my daughter. I was certainly still the mother, but she was much more capable of making her own decisions and of asking questions of others. It was a treat to enjoy being in this new place with her. If part of me had worried that I would feel like a burden to her, a blight on her independent time, there was no evidence that this was the case.

I thought back to my own teenage years. I had a good relationship with both of my parents, but my mother leaned on me in some ways, and I did not want to be her confidante. I wanted to support her, but it was not really my job at that age. I certainly didn't want my own seventeen-year-old to feel that she needed to be responsible for me.

Kate and I walked around the complex and met some of the people she had been friendly with. It was fun to share notes about them, to hear her observations, and to witness her excitement. I felt relieved and happy to be with her, in this place, at this time. And I was grateful that we had created this space, a by-product of her intention to explore and expand her horizons.

Part of my enjoyment in my daughters—being able to be there for them and be there with them—involves spending time together in their spaces, in what they enjoy, in what is difficult. It is an unfathomable treat to get an inside view of what they think about, how they think, what leaves an impression, what they find fun or challenging. This way of knowing them is over-the-top satisfying.

I was trying to feel at ease while also appreciating that something BIG has happened. It is not a screaming "You did it!" kind of moment, like finishing a race. It is a slower, gentler realization that seeps into the pieces of our mother-daughter relationship, a deeper knowing, an expanded trust, a richer bond.

Jwalant and others had warned us to stay inside until 4 p.m. the following day, because it was Holi, a holiday celebrated by people throwing color-filled balloons—mostly reds, yellows, oranges, and gold—at each other. There is no way that we were going to spend our one free day inside, so we decided to walk to Boudhanath, about a half hour away.

We had barely advanced a hundred yards on the mostly dirt path when we became a target. I had imagined that we might be exempt from this treatment, but nope. Rarely has my naiveté smacked me so smartly in the face. We might as well have donned neon signs that screamed: UNARMED FOREIGNERS! No balloons in their hands! Repeat, NO BALLOONS! Come and get 'em!

I wasn't sure how I felt about decorating (admittedly casual) clothes in wet paint. But after a balloon hit me in the head, I realized that I was not so happy, which made me feel old and inflexible. Why couldn't I join in the fracas? But it was not my custom, and with so little time here, I was unprepared to spend any of it in this way.

I sensed that Kate would have been all in, but I couldn't get myself to shift gears so quickly. The slow pace of my time in the mountains still informed my sensibility. To avoid feeling even more grouchy, we opted to take a taxi to Boudha.

Fortunately, Kate had become a proficient bargainer in her twelve days in Nepal, and she negotiated the taxi fare. The difference in price was minor, but haggling was clearly expected and respected, and I was glad to see her so comfortable with it.

In the past, she had been reluctant to ask questions of new people or initiate conversation, nudging someone else to do it. What a lovely way to see her growth.

An enormous stupa, standing 118 feet high, its eyes facing out, is a landmark and a UNESCO World Heritage Site. There are many myths about how and when it was constructed (it dates back to 590). We walked around several times (clockwise, since only in this direction is one's karma improved).

At the open-air stores that ring the area, we found wraparound pants that tied at the waist to bring home for Gale and a few other goodies before taking lunch on the second level. From our perch, we watched people—some with pastel yellow and red on their clothes and hair—walking around below. The interior sacred area, however, seemed to be free of balloons.

*The Boudhanath Stupa is a UNESCO world heritage site, and was
a safe haven from flying color-filled balloons on Holi.*

Later in the day, during a guided tour of downtown Kathmandu,
Kate saw people from her course. Their blond hair was splotched with
hues of ocher and gold, and their clothing was covered with paint. "Isn't
it great!" they exclaimed. Their delight made me realize that others, in
a different frame of mind, were able to fully enjoy this high-spirited
holiday. What a release it must be for people living here to let loose and
pummel others in a sanctioned way.

We have absolutely no equivalent in the States. Even on Hallow-
een, throwing eggs or squirting shaving cream is frowned upon. I far
preferred the gaiety of the Nepalese Holi, which was inclusive and
fun. Kate had been a good sport in going along with what made me

comfortable. How serendipitous to be here on this special day, when it was certainly not business as usual.

Kate and I spent a day in Bhaktapur, known for its copious, intricate wood carvings. We were able to lunch on a second level once again, with a view of the square below where we could watch women in bold colors coming to market.

Strings of little sidewalk shops were filled to overflowing with Pepsi and Coca-Cola bottles and instruments of all kinds.

Drinking in the view from our perch for lunch.

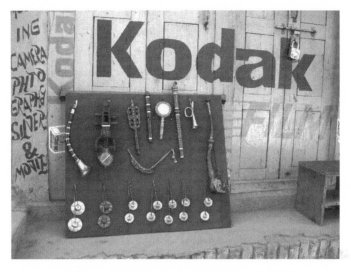

I would have been intrigued to hear what these sounded like,
but regardless, I was drawn to how they looked.

It was extremely hot, and suddenly Kate didn't feel well. We returned to the hotel so she could take a much-needed nap. I embarked on an expedition to find Tylenol and was eventually able to come up with some tablets from a tiny storefront.

We were headed to Bhutan the next morning, chasing happiness and a view of the mountainous country that prioritizes it, for the next three days. From there, we would be routed back through Kathmandu, where we would spend a day before our flight home in the evening.

I appreciated the intensity of the energy in the city, although it took a bit of adjusting. People were striving, connecting, struggling, but interacting, too. The complex weave of commerce, religious commitment, and tourist activity was charged and, to me, compelling.

We were awakened at 4 a.m. by tourists who must have been eager to get on their flight. Otherwise, what could they have been so freaking cheerful about at that hour?

KATE: *Journal excerpt,* 3/8, 9 *p.m.:* I finally got sick today. Nothing too terrible, just some pretty extreme lightheadedness and a fever. It could have been much worse. I managed to sleep most of it off in a two-hour nap.

Gretchen Rubin was definitely right: Good health doesn't exactly add to one's happiness, but bad health absolutely decreases one's happiness. It was hard to be feeling bad in a place where I have such limited time. Ah well, karma.

MEG: In the Nepali airport, we spotted two policemen heading toward the men's room, arm in arm. Kate and I just stared at them (in that way you do when you're trying not to stare), so unusual was this sight. In Nepal it is natural to see men being affectionate with one another, but it had not occurred to us that this demonstrative custom would extend to their police. A charming and unexpected start to the trip.

After a couple of hours, we were herded into another area, where we were to continue to wait. I tried not to get annoyed, but we had only three days in Bhutan, and I didn't want to waste a single second. It was not quite lunchtime when we got the word to board. Could have used that time to sleep in a little longer, but such is the nature of travel. The flight, in a small but not tiny airplane, took only an hour before we landed in a clearing in this mountainous country.

We were collected from the airport by our guide, Mr. Lal, and our driver, Mr. Lassi. They wore traditional Bhutanese menswear: a gho of lovely, muted, multicolored fabric, with Mr. Lal also sporting dressy oxfords and knee socks. (A gho is a tailored, knee-length robe that is large-cuffed, belted at the waist, and worn over a shirt.)

Women wear a jacket and long skirt, together called a kira. I was tempted to buy one, until I realized that it was more practical to settle for a tiny version that would fit over a wine bottle, a satisfying reminder.

Mr. Lal hiccupped extremely loudly and seemingly out of nowhere, a habit that made me want to giggle, a tendency I had to struggle to control.

The newish car was immaculate, in contrast to the worn vehicles common in Nepal. Our ride through the jagged Bhutanese mountains was at once dramatically beautiful and starkly quiet. The new roads were banked and well paved. It was all so different from the chaos of Kathmandu that we were a bit disoriented.

I wonder if they appreciate the fact that these new roads are banked.

These three temples, symbolically located at the convergence of these waters, are side by side, representing Islam, Hinduism, and Buddhism.

With a population of only about 700,000, Bhutan was unlikely to feel crowded. But even as we approached the city of Paro, the landscape was sparse in the valley between mountains. Our hotel was only several years old, and our spacious room boasted a couch, bottled water waiting on the coffee table, and a large, tiled bathroom with an enormous square showerhead. The best description of our feelings would be culture shock.

KATE: *Journal excerpt, 3/9, 9:37 a.m.:* We've been at the airport since 5:45 this morning, but our flight has been delayed until 10ish/ TBD. I'm cultivating patience, but Bhutan is calling my name! Buddhism is right: I had expectations, they're not being met, and it's taking away from my happiness! Ah.

KATE: *Journal excerpt,* 9:50 *p.m.*: It is absolutely stunning here, and even the flight was breathtaking. It could not be more different from Kathmandu. The air is clean, the roads are quiet, everything is of beautiful quality. Things are much more formal here: Our guide, Mr. Lal, always opens doors for us, and most people still wear traditional dress.

They do seem like a happy bunch, though! Mr. Lal is always smiling and in good spirits. He warned us at the beginning that nobody's perfect, that he would try to answer all our questions but might not be able to. He'd find the answer and report back. So sweet.

We had a packed day. The museum, and then "The Fortress," and then a really old temple. Tomorrow we hike to Tiger's Nest, which I am so pumped about.

Walking around Paro felt like culture shock after Kathmandu: barely any people, doors on all the stores, and fixed prices! It's nice dealing with the people in stores, who are all so pleasant.

Buddhism is totally integrated into the culture. There are prayer wheels everywhere, and mandala-type paintings depicting various Buddhist concepts. I wonder if Gross National Happiness, or living as a Buddhist nation, really does have an effect on citizens' happiness. Is simple living what makes people here happier? Is it the beautiful scenery? Is it the heavy integration of Buddhism into society? And most importantly, how happy are they, really?

MEG: Phalluses—symbols of protection and good fortune—rule here. Who wouldn't want a footlong penis on either side of the front door?

One doorway even sported phalluses the size of the door itself. We're talking six-foot-tall matching penises.

Think about it. What every mother and her adolescent daughter want to view together, right? There is no pretending you didn't see it. Very tastefully painted, of course, but our eyes still popped out of our freaking heads. Shops sold phallus keychains, T-shirts, "junk" just hanging out everywhere. We had thought that Florence was a gas, with its packets of penis-shaped pasta, but this was a whole other level of devotion.

I spotted a tiny brass dragon in one shop and decided to buy it. I knew we might see more elsewhere, as the dragon figures prominently on the flag and in the culture, but who knew if I would see another miniature dragon like this. "I'm just feelin' it," I said to Kate. (I have a penchant for miniatures, always have, especially miniatures that actually work and operate like their full-size counterparts.)

Saved myself a thousand words here.

Farther down the street, near our designated meeting place with Mr. Lal, we stopped into a very touristy shop that offered a myriad of phallus keychains, T-shirts, all manner of penile profiling. We looked them over, but we were just shopped out. "Just not feelin' it, Kate," I said. And then we both burst out laughing at the unintended double entendre.

We were still chuckling as we walked out to the car, where Mr. Lal regarded us for a moment, and then said, "The phallus, right?"

I started to protest that we were not shocked, being *waaaay* more sophisticated than that, of course. Except, well, we *were* joking about it, and protesting would just drive his point home (if you know what I mean).

So I just ended up agreeing. Yep, guess we're just like every mother-daughter pair to come through here, and we are in fact commenting on the phalluses. Mr. Lal is allowed a LOL on us. Good fun for all, though I imagine they might get tired of this "intercourse."

It is striking to see penis heads on random countryside fountains and door handles. I wondered how casual phallus decorations everywhere affect people's sex lives, and how they regard intimacy in general. These are not questions for our young guide and driver, who seem to be in their late twenties and feel good about scoring these jobs. Although I talk to people about intimate aspects of their lives in my work as a psychotherapist, this is very different. I will have to curb my curiosity.

Bhutan is gradually allowing tourism. So that the country is not overwhelmed by it, flights from Nepal arrived only three days a week. The authorities are strict about what tourists see, and in our short stay here, every aspect of our visit was chosen for us: where we stayed, what sights we saw, and even where and what we ate. Restaurants often offered buffets of certain foods. Kate and I enjoyed it, but it felt odd to have so many of our choices made for us.

Our guide has definite ideas about where and when to take photos.

I knew that some people stayed for a longer time, and that they were able to get out into the country and even stay with people on a farm. The couple who sat at the next table at dinner were traveling for several months and were planning to spend two weeks in Bhutan. I envied this luxury, an opportunity to get to know so much more about the land and the people.

A photo of the Tiger's Nest monastery, built into a steep cliffside, was partially responsible for propelling me on this trip. The way that it so beautifully blended with the surrounding mountains captivated me.

See what I mean about catapulting me toward this place?

*The spinning of the prayer wheels is a way of life,
completely integrated into the day.*

Prayer wheels lined our way up the nearly two-hour hike, and Mr. Lal did not miss a single opportunity to spin them.

Even as we drew close to the ancient site, it was difficult to see how we could navigate our way across the divide to get there. Only as we were nearly upon it did we see the tiny bridge that closed the gap between two seemingly disconnected peaks.

We were not allowed to bring cameras inside, and so we surrendered our packs upon entry to the ornate monastery, which had been redone following a 1998 fire. Considered the birthplace of Bhutanese Buddhism, this is one of the most sacred places in the country. Its seclusion, and the effort required to get there, sets it apart. Though many people make this very doable pilgrimage, it can be a challenge for older people, who rely on donkeys to make most of the trip. The spectacular views add to the gravity and majesty of its power, and I felt like I was living in history, a part of this ancient culture.

The next day, having visited several monasteries and museums (which featured pieces from monasteries), it was a welcome change to see the enormous golden Buddha and site still under construction, followed by the farmer's market and zoo. The sitting Buddha is sixty-nine feet tall, one of the tallest in the world. (Roughly 75 percent of the people in Bhutan are Buddhists, with Hindus making up around 22 percent. The remainder follow folk religions.)

At the zoo we were able to see the country's national animal, the takin. It is a shy, hairy, reverse-horned beast that mostly stays in forested areas, except during the flood season, when it moves to higher ground.

The charming myth about this animal is that the fifteenth-century lama Drukpa Kunley was supposed to perform a miracle at the end of a feast, and he put the head of a goat onto the body of a cow. The takin does confound easy categorization, and is thus labeled *budorcas*

Kate thoughtfully pointing out the Buddha behind her lest we miss it.

The takin really is a most curious looking beast.

taxicolor (meaning badger-colored, ox-like gazelle). I loved the sign that warned us not to tease the animals. I made a mental note not to tell them any jokes.

The massive farmer's market was housed in a covered concrete building. We were left to wander here on our own for a couple of hours, enjoying the colorful variety of vegetables and the sight of people shopping for their homes and for the hotels.

Our three days passed in the blink of an eye. On the morning of our departure, we were picked up before dawn by our trusty guide and driver. It was the one time they were almost late. Dressed in Western clothing, they were joking with one another and listening to rock music on the radio. I was surprised to see them like this, but glad too, relieved that they could relax. I wished we could have evoked this response in them, but I don't think they would have allowed it before now. They took their positions very seriously.

We used our ten-hour layover in Kathmandu to relax in our hotel room. We also scooted out to Yasmine's store, where I scored a couple of samples to take home. I bought a fitted black-and-orange-striped dress, with complementary dotted panels and a lovely, flowy drape. A beautifully made, dichroic blue/green jacket and pants seemed tailored for me. Although they were not at all my usual style, how could I not buy them as well?

KATE: *Journal excerpt, 3/10, 6 p.m.:* We drove out of Paro this morning to hike up to Taktsang Monastery, or Tiger's Nest. It was a fairly intense and steep hike, about an hour and forty-five minutes up, including the time we took to take pictures.

The prayer flags are ubiquitous, creating beautiful shapes and patterns.

Unusual pathway with Kate and Mr. Lal in the distance.

The mountains and untouched grandeur of Bhutan continue to stun me. It seems like there are more prayer flags than buildings, and both only add to the beauty!

The temples within the monastery were intense for us as visitors, and the respect shown by Buddhists is huge. Our guide prostrated at least ten times while he was with us and spun every prayer wheel in sight.

On the way down we stopped at the Taktsang Jahhang, a small teahouse. Our cups and plate of biscuits were never empty. The service was so prompt, and the people were overwhelmingly polite at the teahouse (and everywhere in Bhutan).

After the hike down, we stopped by some ruins, had lunch, and started on the drive to Thimphu, about an hour away from Paro.

Another beautiful temple on the way, Tamchog Lhakhang, was built by Thangtong Gyalpo in the fifteenth century. What I really loved was the story of the bridge that approached it.

The original bridge (also created by Thangtong Gyalpo) was made of huge iron links, but it was washed away in a flood a couple of years ago. Some of the links were recovered and built into the new bridge.

Those iron links still lined the bottoms and sides of the bridge, along with prayer flags, of course. The huge, green mountains surrounding it, the clear river below flowing freely over the rocks—all of it was incredible, a perfect moment.

When we arrived in Thimphu, Mr. Lal advised getting a good night's sleep after an exhausting day.

My mom and I took a second to breathe—then headed out to a shopping mall next door to the hotel. It had five floors, each one with about six stores. We just walked around, seeing what there was to see. It seemed a stark contrast with the rest of the country, but I guess we'll see what the city is really like tomorrow.

We also saw a woman entering the temple opposite. It is remarkable how many of these temples remain active, serving the people.

Coming out of my experience at Kopan, I was wary of having Buddhism pushed on me. Ironically, we're visiting ten temples a day and walking city streets lined with prayer wheels! The culture is fascinating and well preserved, and I'm taking in as much as I possibly can every second.

We started out by seeing a large stupa in Thimphu valley, and then we went to one of the largest sitting statues of Buddha in the world. We walked nearby for a while and took in the views of the valley. Then we saw Bhutan's first nunnery (looks very similar to a monastery). There were lots of people there, taking the day to pray.

We went to a zoo in the morning, where we saw a takin, the national animal of Bhutan. There were also barking deer and somba deer, which were all very cute. After lunch we saw the Tashichho Dzong, which houses the center of the national government and the central monastic body. It is right near the king's palace, which is actually quite modest. We were told not to take pictures or look directly at the palace; you have to peek as you walk by or the guards will come speak to you!

In the afternoon, we went to the farmer's market, which was huge! It's where everybody does their shopping for produce, cheese, fish, incense, and similar items.

People truly adore their royalty here, and there were photos everywhere:
inside our hotels, and often on the streets as pictured here.

We also shopped at a handicraft emporium and walked around the center of Thimphu. Our guide told us there wasn't anything to see, and that wasn't too much of an exaggeration. Just one main road with some pretty average shops.

Now I'm just waiting for dinner and any adventures that remain before our long journey home, starting at 4 a.m.

MEG: The dirty young guy seated next to me on the plane demanded my headphones expectantly, as if I owed him. I handed them over and pointed out some empty seats a couple of rows up. I was relieved when he took advantage of that observation and moved. I felt bad to have hesitated, frustrated to be in this position at all, annoyed that I questioned myself.

The way home felt endless. I kept falling asleep during the movie *Marilyn* and then waking up and rewinding. I managed to repeat this pattern four times before I actually finished the film. Kate, mostly awake, seemed entertained at how many times I could pull the *Groundhog Day* routine.

KATE: *Journal entry from Kopan teachings:* Happiness is created within. Happiness coming from outside is fleeting.

All actions in life for all beings are done with the motivation to be happy.

People have a higher intelligence and therefore happiness is harder to achieve. Society tells us this is where true happiness comes from.

Buddhists say you can be completely happy. You still grieve, but it's different. You need wisdom, and to remember the good things, to appreciate life.

People try to change the outside world, but you can only change the inside.

All sentient beings are equal, all with the same potential.

Buddhist definition of happiness:

Mind is completely peaceful, not disturbed or agitated by what happens. Contentment can lead to short-term happiness. We need to practice it to train the mind. Meditation is mental training. Wisdom simply means awareness of reality.

Lama Zopa Rinpoche said: "Attachment is like honey on a razor's edge; it looks like pleasure but offers only pain. Everything depends on how you use your mind. The way to solve the problems in your life is to open your heart to others."

KATE: *Journal excerpt on returning home:* Happiness has still been on my mind, even though (as predicted) I haven't journaled as much as I'd hoped since being home.

So what is my personal recipe for happiness? Just as the great thinkers of the world have disagreed about what brings happiness, the different parts of myself continue to question and re-question what brings me happiness.

Gretchen Rubin, author of *The Happiness Project*, theorizes that the best way to increase one's happiness is to remove the sources of unhappiness. For me, procrastination absolutely drives me crazy, so the challenge I gave myself at home was "Do it now." The satisfaction I get from accomplishing a task and not having it hang over my head is enormous. I absolutely feel an increase in my happiness when I get my homework done before 11 p.m., or put away that pesky load of laundry.

This same goal had presented itself entirely differently in Nepal. I knew my time in Nepal was limited, and I wanted to soak up every moment I had there. Instead of being terrified to board a Nepali bus— so crowded I couldn't see out the windows—I just went for it, knowing that the moment was fleeting.

So whether I'm taking the dog for a quick stroll or having a third piece of homemade bread in a Buddhist monastery, taking hold of every moment has become essential to me. It leads me to live passionately, which is exactly what I want.

It would have been cheaper to take a weekend course in western Massachusetts, but I wouldn't have experienced the absolute terror of being alone in a foreign country, knowing there wasn't a simple escape even if I hated every minute of it. I also wouldn't have had the overwhelming sense of pride and pleasure of finishing the course, and even enjoying it. And I definitely wouldn't have had to try to communicate with people who don't speak my language. Or navigate my way back home from the heart of a foreign city.

But because I threw myself into it without a safety net, I had the privilege of taking all those risks. I enjoy travel because I like visiting new places, but I love travel because it gives me the opportunity to accomplish something I never thought possible.

Challenge is essential to happiness. The feeling of hard work and (hopefully) success is one that can't be replicated. The risk of failure is always there, but growth is inevitable. Without challenge, I (and, I believe, people in general) become bored. Happiness stems from experience, and being bored is not experience!

I learned a lot from the course I took on Buddhism, but I learned even more about myself through the people I met. Human connection is vital to happiness. During my first night at Kopan monastery, I felt more scared and more alone than I have in a long time—and it's no coincidence that I felt both. Once I started to meet people, I got really excited about being in Nepal: learning how to barter from Ross, the boisterous Australian, or playing hacky sack with Mai from Denmark. My most memorable moments were the interactions I had with people.

The principle of human connection holds true at home as well. My day can be turned around by a simple phone call from a friend or a smile from a stranger. This isn't to say that I don't ever want or need to be alone, but human interaction hugely contributes to my happiness.

So there it is, Kate Stafford's equation for happiness: challenge plus moment-seizing plus people equal :D !

The more I explore my happiness, the more I realize how important it is. With each answer I find, three more questions sprout. I guess I'll be chasing happiness for a while!

KATE: *Reflections from four years later:* Looking back on this trip, it is easy to identify it as one of the most influential experiences of my youth. I would have taken a drastically different path had I not traveled to Nepal and Bhutan at age seventeen.

I finished out my senior year of high school and decided to take a gap year before heading to college. After working through the summer and fall, I traveled to South Africa, Namibia, Ireland, Scotland, England, Germany, France, Croatia, Hungary, and Slovenia. By the end of my trip, I had so fallen in love with being abroad that I decided against attending the small New England college where I had been accepted in order to apply to universities in the UK. I took another year off to complete the necessary exams and spent half of that time working and traveling in New Zealand.

Now I've completed my second year at the University of Edinburgh and will finish my undergraduate degree in philosophy and psychology here. My time in Nepal and my senior project sparked an interest in positive psychology and happiness, so much so that I'm working to get a degree in learning about it.

My travels and studies are just the most obviously influenced parts of my life. As I reflected four years ago, I learned more from the people and places than I did from the course on Buddhism. I experienced independence in a way I never had before—and in a way that, I believe, is unique to travel. I still chase after the thrill of discovering a new place and making it mine, the freeing helplessness of getting lost and depending on the kindness of strangers to find your way.

I believe strongly in trusting myself, backing myself to conquer any challenge, and challenging myself to live passionately and truly in the pursuit of happiness.

MEG: Our time away has changed us both. Three weeks doesn't sound like such a long time. What's the big deal? Why were these three weeks spilling over into the rest of my life?

They popped up in unexpected places and unanticipated times, waking me at 4 a.m. and stealing my concentration midafternoon. I seemed unable to contain them in photographs or a journal. My thoughts were like brightly colored fabric that feels light as air and floats from your hands with the slightest breeze.

(Kate was also having a hard time concentrating. Much later, she told me that she had been feeling less than motivated about finishing her senior year of high school after returning, but a trusted teacher who had had a similar experience talked her through it.)

I know that it was not just the formal learning that shaped Kate's experience. She described the people she met from Switzerland, Germany, India, Denmark, Australia, and Ireland. She explored Kathmandu and Boudhanath. She learned how to bargain, hail a cab, and negotiate the fare. She sat on the floor for hours at a stretch and watched monks debate in Tibetan. She listened to the music of Nepali weddings celebrated and watched festival lights being hung. She merged with the cars, cows, scooters, and dogs that flowed through the swirling fishbowl of movement on the streets of Kathmandu.

And she felt at home, even in that faraway Himalayan valley, years younger than everyone else, and she was herself. She was respected for who she was, for her ideas, for how she expressed herself and listened to others. Her world swelled to include these people, her view of what is possible, and the myriad ways that people can and do live their lives. She seemed quite pleased about the ways in which that view did not fit into her previous understanding.

I realized that I am just as gratified. I have been reunited with my own passion for being in a new place and for seeing it unfold slowly through the trek. It will take some time to fully appreciate what we have brought home from the mountains and streets of Kathmandu and

Bhutan. There is no deadline by which we must absorb it all. I can let it sift through in its own time, letting the light fall on each angle as it presents itself in the kaleidoscope of experience.

I treasured this time with Kate. It created a new way to be together, nurturing the connection with others, within ourselves, and with each other.

Section Two

Colombia, 2013–2015

Wherever you go becomes a part of you somehow.

—ANITA DESAI,
CLEAR LIGHT OF DAY

MEG: After Kate's trip to Nepal and Bhutan (and her subsequent visits to South Africa, among other locales), you might think that I was well versed in dealing with my children's offbeat jaunts. But nothing could have prepared me for the heart-stopping plans of my older daughter following grad school.

In September 2013, Gale informed us that she could not fathom getting a traditional teaching position right away (hmm, detecting a family pattern here). Instead, she was headed to one of the most violent places on earth—rural Colombia—where she would be working with a nongovernment organization. Until this moment, I had studiously stayed out of her research, waiting as she interviewed with various organizations and hoping that her interest in this particular program would somehow fade with the waning summer light. Nope.

I should have expected something like this. Almost since birth, Gale has been a great communicator, especially when it comes to the Spanish language and to Latin America. But there's another layer to my firstborn: her extreme extraversion. She engages anyone and everyone, and she always has.

She was the kind of toddler who spent transatlantic flights entertaining nearby passengers by offering them tiny fistfuls of mini pretzels and her homemade macaroni necklace. At our annual family camp outings in Acadia National Park in Maine, she thought nothing of heading off on a kayaking adventure with another family (when she had rolled her eyes at the idea of doing a favorite hike with us).

Her mastery of Spanish started with our trip to visit my mother in Mexico when she was thirteen. After a week, she could already connect in that language—but she was fascinated with every aspect of the culture, from food to art to politics. After a scant two years of instruction, and shedding her fear of grammatical faux pas, she could easily communicate her ideas. In high school she spent five weeks living with a family in Costa Rica (where her mail was addressed to "the store across the street from the church near X street," with mixed delivery results).

During college, Gale worked as a camp counselor for seven weeks in Peru. Our first international mother-daughter adventure involved my scooping her up for a week that included a magical visit to Machu Picchu and a memorable bus ride to her host family in Chimbote, in the north, with the ocean on one side and endless sand dunes on the other.

Stints in Chile and Argentina followed. By the time Gale had attained a concentration in teaching Spanish, with a fifth year to complete her master's degree, Duke and I were well on our way to learning how to stretch the cord between continents and various means of communication.

Chile, it turns out, was a huge influence on what would follow. Gale spent her last month there studying a largely indigenous school. Her coursework focused on the effects of human rights violations on education during the country's seventeen-year dictatorship.

So Gale was in some ways perfectly positioned to go to Colombia and put herself on the line for the cause of peace. But it would not be straightforward or easy (for me, anyway) to accept that this work, important though it was, would be worth what I perceived to be the tremendous risks she was taking. It would turn out to be another lesson in negotiating our intertwined spirals of connection and independence.

GALE: I wasn't necessarily looking for Colombia; Colombia came to me.

I had gone to grad school to get my degree in high school Spanish teaching; education is my biggest passion, and I went for Spanish because of my love for the language and cultures I have gotten to know. After a singularly tumultuous year of student teaching, however, I was looking for an experience that would be completely different, prior to teaching full time.

I went for a walk with a brilliant, compassionate friend who asked me where I would ideally be in a year and what I would be doing. After pondering for a bit, I concluded that I would most want to be doing a one- to two-year program in a Spanish-speaking location—hopefully doing something important or interesting. I was still receiving emails from Fellowship of Reconciliation, an organization (somewhere in Latin American, I seemed to recall) connected to Janice, one of my high school Spanish teachers. The message included a project progress update, a poignant quote from Dr. Martin Luther King Jr., and, most notably, a quote by Janice.

I thought to myself, "It's a sign!" and applied on the spot. I went to Bogotá for a weeklong "mutual discernment process" (interview) a couple of months later, and it was all forward from there. In retrospect, it would have been prudent to have had a better understanding of the work before I jumped in, but I'm still glad I did it.

I spent a few days in Bogotá before making my way to La Unión, deep in the far northwestern countryside, where I would spend the next nine months. (Later I returned to Bogotá to be part of the team on the ground for the following nine.)

Colombia is home to the longest-standing conflict in the western hemi-sphere, evolving over time but largely centering on disputes over the fertile, coca-growing land. Many civilians have been displaced or killed during these disputes.

The main umbrella groups are the military (among the top recipients of US military aid, and widely understood to be corrupt), the paramil-itaries (essentially mercenaries and vigilantes, these are the principal narco-traffickers who, more recently, clear the way for international mining and fracking companies), and the guerrillas (who ostensibly started out defending the general population but swiftly became their own brand of often-senseless and misdirected violence).

All three groups, in varying combinations over time, make for a volatile political environment. Ironically, they operate in the midst of a stunning land whose people are some of the brightest, warmest, and kindest anywhere.

In the midst of it all is a displaced group, in the upper northwest corner of the country, which has intentionally opted out of the conflict. After significant persecution (including assassinations, massacres, and multiple displacements, primarily by the military and paramilitaries), the community members teamed up with recognized social leaders, wrote a manifesto, and officially declared themselves La Comunidad de Paz (the Peace Community).

As a part of their long-term safety plan, in 1998 the Community invited international accompaniers, including Fellowship of Reconciliation (called FOR, and later FOR Peace Presence) to serve as a part of their protection.

FOR, along with other groups with international connections, would act as a visible presence, living in the community and literally accompanying its members from place to place. They would thereby act as witnesses and megaphones about what they observe and learn about the movements of the armed actors. This, along with other safety measures, significantly decreased the threats to the Peace Community.

FOR Peace Presence accompaniers do not impart advice; they simply relay whatever they observe, so the armed actors know the world is watching. If these forces rely on the silence of anonymity to act without regard for human life, international accompaniment effectively disables that silence.

MEG: I have long known that fear can worm its way into any narrative, hijacking an otherwise perfectly lovely time. Fear has its place, and can be vital for self-preservation, but I, selfishly perhaps, do not like it to get in the way of fun. I therefore have become skilled at finding effective means to squeeze uncomfortable feelings into smaller packages, leaving more room for laughter, adventure, and love.

When Gale made clear that she was pursuing this position in Colombia, I'm sure my eyes grew wide and my pulse quickened. The Colombia I grew up hearing about was home to drug cartels, violence, and unpredictability. Gale's reassurance about more recent changes did little to erase these images. Research showed that FOR was an established organization and that the violence was more than a decade in the past. I had to remind myself that a decade to me read like "last week," whereas to her it seemed long ago, when she was still a child.

I heard her excitement about how impressive her week of training had been, how well-thought-out and executed. I heard about the security measures in place and her eagerness to be speaking Spanish all the time.

I considered the amount of walking this assignment would involve, her skill at mediation, and how much she is nurtured by being in a new culture.

I reflected on our recent five-mile walks together and saw how important this transition was for her. After an excruciating year of graduate school, she was thirsty for something nonacademic. Despite her passion for teaching, she could not settle into a position just yet, not with the world beckoning, inviting her to connect to people in a different way.

And, although she would be living a twelve- to sixteen-hour bus ride from Bogotá, she would have access to cell phones and internet (when they were working), and bright blue T-shirts that bear the name of their organization.

When she walked with community members, she would be getting to know them, and they would learn about her. She would see what they eat and what their favorite dances are. She would learn how to make puns in Spanish and how to spot a pig in the path when it is belly deep in mud. She would find out what is important to these people and what their dreams look like. Spending a year in this community, she would become a part of it. I knew that she loved to immerse herself in a situation and live it fully, from the inside out. We would look for her posts, photographs, and stories.

And I? I would start searching for affordable flights to Bogotá—and a quicker-than-sixteen-hour route to her village from there. I could hardly wait.

GALE: email excerpt, December 13, 2013: I've had my first accompaniment trip! We received the petition for accompaniment a couple of Sundays ago. After our risk analysis (*análisis de riesgo*), we were ready to head out on Wednesday to La Esperanza ("The Hope"), a village a handful of hours away, to visit the Community members there who were doing a livestock census.

I was a little confused when I learned that the Community actually consists of at least eleven small villages spread over large stretches of land. How could it be a community if it's stretched out so big? The simplest response is to think of the Community as clusters of actors under the same umbrella organization. (Members can even be married to nonmembers.) One of the things that attracted me to this program is the amount of walking necessary. In each part of the application process, I had been asked about my relationship with walking, and I had assured everybody that mine was hearty and positively delightful (with the exception of one defiant/pouty twelve-mile jaunt I took to a friend's house during high school). The only thing that can interfere with the great joy and solace of walking is hiking uphill—which is exactly what we were about to do.

I credit the brilliant choreographers and dance teachers in my past with how little I fell down, but, really, it was only a matter of time. The muddy trek was laced with roots in the most inconvenient places.

I like to think that I have some elegance with my gait, and consider walking to be something I'm capable of, having learned at the age of two. So I started out picking my way around, reveling in the beauty of the place, and snap-snapping some photos for the folks at home.

But throw in some serious ascension, and maybe slap on a little mud, and then I get crabby (internally, anyway, because there was no way in hell I was about to start complaining). Then I get red and turn into a total sweat factory. Rather than being helpful, I felt I was dragging them down, requiring more care and attention than I would have liked to attract.

So after a few literal ups and downs, I learned some lessons I'm excited to share with you all:

1. When life offers you *mula,* take the damn mula. I hated that I needed a break, but I did. When you are holding people up and your shining colleague (who is lankier than the mule he is comically perched on) offers to switch, check your pride at the door and take that offer fast (if begrudgingly).

2. Mula doesn't mean "moolah," but it's funny when everybody shouts that all the time. And while a chorus of people all going "¡MULA! ¡MULAMULA!" is as funny as it sounds, it's also remarkably effective for getting the mula to do things like move, move faster, and move in a different way.

3. When you're on the mula, you'll grunt "¡MULA!" too. You just will.

4. Basic mula motion. Keep the reins loose (as anything else means stop). Right means right, left means left, "MULA" means go, and kick-kick means, "Seriously, go (even if it's not convenient for Your Muliness)." And hang the heck on.

5. Riding on a mula may scare the crap out of you. Have you ever seen a mule walk up a mountain? Neither had I. But it turns out they can do it, up absolutely terrifying pitches. Hold tight and crush your thighs as hard as you can into the raging pack of muscles. Keeping the bridle loose and out of the Stop position (to allow their heads and necks to surge forward) is a bit of a challenge for the short-armed among us.

6. You may surprise yourself with a mula. Turns out I'm not bad at riding! I'm reserving judgment until I can hold on more easily to the front of the saddle, which the Colombians do casually, with only one hand on the reins.

7. If you're going to fall off your mula, do it in slo-mo. Not when you manage to hang on when the mula unexpectedly launches itself over a stream. Nah, fall when you duck down to avoid some branches and then slide in slow motion down . . . the side . . . of the animal . . .

8. We really do need each other. Upon picking me up off the ground, the person in charge of all of the livestock got quite the kick out of this: "Ah, haha, but you made me laugh."

9. "Great, glad it was hilarious," said my pride.

10. "No, no, I'm laughing because you're fine. And, boy, was that funny." He grinned. He was spot-on as a gracious teacher and

humbling reminder that pride is not all that. They needed us, and we needed their help. So I laughed, got back on the mula, and continued home without further incident.

MEG: The people of La Unión, and in La Holandita, have become Gale's connection to the outside world and have become her family. I am both grateful and a little wistful. I want for her to feel rooted, especially in such a turbulent place. She relies on her colleagues in a way that determines everyone's safety. Whatever pangs I feel for her youth are swept away by the need for her to be fully present and in touch with what is. I had not before needed to feel this level of trust, but now it is the best (and only) way forward.

A family friend in the military assured us that accompaniment really does protect the community. The military, paramilitaries, and guerrillas know that should they cross the line and put lives in jeopardy, there will be serious consequences, and this understanding is achieved without physical force. He is a direct and straightforward person, and so I found his reassurance meaningful. I felt my shoulders relax and my breath deepen.

I always want to convey my confidence in Gale, her situation, and her judgment. The land demands it, and the people are counting on it, as are her colleagues.

They communicate with their headquarters in Bogotá and monitor the armed actors' whereabouts and movements on a daily basis. But I don't know exactly what that means. How frequently does communication happen? What is the process for emergencies? What constitutes an emergency? What is it like to shift back and forth from everyday life to accompanying people to the hospital or to visit other people, to celebrate or to mourn?

I know that Gale and her colleagues very much want to be there. Their generosity and conviction is moving and striking. They are voting with their feet in lending their support to people they have never met, in a land in which they have never before lived.

I wonder sometimes where this passion came from, but does that even matter? Gale is living what she believes.

GALE: email excerpt, May 31, 2014: One of the things we get to do is meet with local authorities to remind them that we're here, watching. We share some of our recent preoccupations and essentially renew ourselves as thorns in their sides. This helps keep the army (and the paramilitaries with which they collaborate) on their toes and the Community safer.

A few weeks ago, we had an overwhelming couple of days with a delegation, including a trip to meet with the 17th Brigade, the most wide-reaching troops in the area.

The Colombian army receives a shocking amount of aid from the United States, but this particular brigade doesn't, because it was found responsible for a 2005 massacre of eight people, including three children and Community members. FOR, which had lived with the Community since the late 1990s, was called to be witnesses of the army's involvement, and it was largely due to their documentation that the 17th Brigade lost US funding. This is perhaps one of the most tangible effects accompaniment can have.

While the military leadership has since changed, there is now an illegal army base close to Community land, and the 17th Brigade remains the most notable legal armed group in the area.

In advance of our meeting, we prepared our four visiting delegates, including the International FOR representative to the UN, a board member of the School of the Americas Watch (this organization opposes the School of the Americas, a US entity that essentially trains all manner of Latin American assassins and elite army groups), an SoAW volunteer, and a member of Amnesty International in Germany.

My colleague Kaya facilitated the meeting with the army, and I had the pleasure of translating. As a language-based person and potential aspiring translator, I found this kind of assignment to be a total dream.

There are two approaches to live translation: A speaker can talk in small chunks, which get translated one by one, or they can talk for as long as they want, and the translator does simultaneous translation, talking over them in a fluid stream. I was a bit nervous and asked at the outset that everybody speak in small chunks, so I could accurately portray what they said. Linguistically it was tricky, because I don't have the training. But I was so baffled by what they were saying that I sometimes found it challenging to translate. "*Todos queremos la paz*" ("We all want peace") was one of the tamer things they said, as the four army officials oscillated between lies and twisted inaccuracies. I found that the best approach was to keep as neutral as possible and process later. If I analyzed what they were spouting, I would be unable to relay it at all.

In court cases, translators must swear that they will translate as accurately as possible—but the meaning of "accuracy" can be super subjective. In addition to the plain meaning of words, there's also an emotional component, which can change that meaning. So in order to translate accurately, you really have to empathize with the speaker in order to match the real meaning of their words.

And that was the wildest part of this meeting. In trying to listen closely—especially when they didn't speak in short chunks and just kept talking—the words began tumbling out of my mouth. It was hard not to feel a little like the army myself. Our delegates asked some tricky questions, and we had made it difficult for the 17th, but after the meeting, I was shaken. I was surprised and confused by how they twisted laws and Inter-American Court orders, and I was distracted by their lack of sympathy for the Peace Community, which wants nothing to do with the conflict.

They were looking me in the eye and telling me they were protecting everybody. But how many of their mines had gone off recently? How much guerrilla action had their troops attracted? How many people had they personally killed or been ordered to kill?

It was hard to sustain eye contact. Watching them fiddle with their phones or their rings reminded me that they have families and might like sending pictures of cats to their friends. Meeting with the army is wild.

MEG: What was billed as a twelve- to sixteen-hour bus ride from Bogotá to Gale's village was actually an eleven-hour bus ride followed by a seven-hour bus ride, followed by a forty-five-minute open-air jeep ride, followed by a two-hour walk through the mud.

As fate would serve it up, her first day in the Community was Thanksgiving. She had expected to be in Bogotá, putting together a holiday meal with her colleagues there. Instead, because she was spending the night in Apartado before heading up to the community, she made *arroz con leche* (a sweet rice pudding) and lit tiny birthday candles to acknowledge Hanukkah (which coincided that year!).

Gale called us just as my husband was putting the bird on the table and as I was pulling trays of heavenly casseroles from our oven. I ran back and forth, listening as she and Kate exchanged updates. As we corralled our group of sixteen to the table, I abandoned hope of meaningful phone conversation and consoled myself with the notion of a longer conversation later in the weekend. The enthusiasm at our table made the absence of Gale's contagious laughter even more notable. Hearing her voice even briefly was at once a reassurance and also a reminder of the distance between us.

"This will be life changing," our guests commented. I could only nod silently. They were not wrong, although I cannot know how or where the changes will lead her. I actually don't want to know now. Part of the deliciousness, if I can stand it, is in watching it unfold.

She was reassuring about the security measures that FOR is taking when they decide whether to honor a request for accompaniment. I still don't know the details of how they obtain their information, and I find myself once again at a crossroads, trying to highlight the reassurance of their precaution rather than the fact that there is a need for it.

I'm also reassured that the hospitals are very reputable. Although I'm glad to hear this, and the organization jokes about how past volunteers have put that to the test with good results, I do not want to learn through experience that their perspective is valid. It makes me queasy just hearing it, like we're supposed to prepare for some calamity but we don't know what it is or when. I realized I was hungry for pictures. If I can get a visual, I can start to fill in some of the blanks: who is welcoming, who is shy, what she means when she says it's HUMID (although not unpleasantly hot). Of course, it will remain to be seen how close I can come to understanding her experience. Time to dust off my high school Spanish.

I have learned that I can get from Boston to Medellín in eight hours, with just one stop. Then it's just the seven-hour bus ride, open-air jeep, and a hop-skip in my mud boots to see her new life.

Part of me can't believe that my twenty-three-year-old met with Colombian military leaders. It just doesn't make sense to my adult brain that my child is meeting with people who make decisions about killing other people.

I don't doubt her ability. But it is a stretch to imagine that she and Kaya, her colleague, were negotiating (sometimes close to reprimanding?) these mostly adult men about their roles in the area. It is a full lesson in believing in what you're doing.

In just a few weeks, Gale has already learned about the tight connections within the Community. She is touched and moved by their level of commitment to one another, and by their generosity and curiosity. "Everybody has their people, and they keep them close," she says.

GALE: email excerpt, October 19, 2014: It is a special thing to spend the "one- to two-hour depending on the rain/mud situation and your lil non-*campesino* leggies" walk home, passing people who are either close friends or relatives of those on the mountain.

The most important thing is showing up. When an old, beloved neighbor fell ill one evening, almost every child and at least half of the adults in La Unión showed up to just be there. In reality, only a few were actively doing something to help him. Everybody else was just there.

I have talked with people who have experienced unfathomable trauma, and I am both quieted into reflection about my own upsets and humbled by the trust in connection and desire for understanding.

I have been reminded by my teammates how many different ways there are to connect with people, and to look for the gems that people inevitably have to offer. Above all, conversations that divert from the topic at hand can be unexpected opportunities. Sometimes, impulsiveness is just the thing.

MEG: I felt the urge to nail down my travel plans when Gale had been away for only six weeks. A few phone calls were certainly good. A little email was helpful but could never replace a hug. The connection was not stellar, and most of the residents relied on cell phones instead.

A year would be too long to go without eyeballing the girl. More than anything, I needed to do an on-the-ground assessment of the safety of this whole operation. Not that I could do anything about it, of course. Gale had elected to be there, and the time to protest or request change of any kind had long since passed. But for my own comfort, and my own ability to connect with her in my mind and my heart, I wanted to sniff the air, meet the people, walk the terrain, and get a sense of the place. Then I could hold her in my mind's eye and send her my love, my good feelings, in a more immediate and directed way.

This was of tremendous comfort to me. I began to focus on my own trip rather than on the fact that she would be away for so long. Just knowing that I was going settled me down somewhat. I could anticipate what to bring and gather materials for the Community as part of my way of thanking them for having me as a guest. What would it be like there? Would it feel tense? Full of danger? Were they worried all the time? Were they on guard, vigilant, ready for action? The atmosphere would speak volumes.

GALE: email excerpt, February 15, 2015: It turns out that my first name, Gale, is really hard for Spanish speakers to pronounce, and they rather shy away from using it. So I go by my middle name, which is Virginia. It took me a little while to get used to that, but I now no longer feel like a liar when I introduce myself that way in Spanish, rather than apologetically saying my first name and adding, "but you can call me Virginia if you want." They gratefully sigh, "Virginia" after looks of confusion and hit-or-miss pronunciation of "Gale" ("Gell. Kayo? Kell. Kull. Gull.").

It's probably more confusing for my poor colleagues, who call me Gale but then need to refer to me as Virginia. The Italian accompaniment group, Palomas, was the first to consistently call me "Virgi," which I like and will respond to—it's so fun to have a nickname within a nickname! Little kids saying my name is absolutely adorable ("Bee-HEEN-yah!"), and it allows me to think more robustly about cultivating my Spanish-speaking identity to match all the ways I hear my name.

MEG: My husband remembered that the boots are to prevent snake bites. I recalled only that the boots are for mud. We asked Gale, who confirmed that we are both right.

How convenient of me to forget that little detail about the snakes. If you screen out the risks and the scary bits, you are left with adventure. It's a tricky business sometimes, maintaining this perspective.

My daughter informed me that she has a pair of boots for me. They might be a little big, but that shouldn't matter too much. I am bringing extra pairs of tall socks for her anyway, so I'm sure I'll be all set.

I called my credit card company to let them know when I will be in Colombia. The customer service rep made conversation about the reason for my travel. I began to explain that my daughter is living for a year in a community that is a forty-five-minute open-air jeep ride and a long walk in the mud from the nearest town with a store. I heard a shift in the rep's voice as she responded, "Wow." There was a moment of silence.

"Yeah, it's pretty far out there," I went on. "They're used to it, though. They make that trip every week, because they don't have a refrigerator." I heard her attentive silence, so I continued.

"She's there with two other volunteers [they do get a tiny stipend], living in the community and accompanying them to other communities or wherever they need to go to make sure they are safe. It's just by their presence that they do this, not by any other means."

"You're blowing my mind," said the rep. "I'm living in my comfy home and don't think twice about running down the street to get food or anything for my one-year-old daughter. Wow," she said. "WOW."

I realized that I have begun to take this situation a bit for granted. "She has called it paradise," I continued. "She says it's lush, lush, lush, with lots of delicious, unidentifiable fruits and great food, because she's living among farmers."

In our companionable silence I sensed we were both thinking about how relative our perspectives are. Does she wonder where her one-year-old will be at age twenty-three?

I considered how interdependent people must be there. If they can't just pop off for some eggs or flour, they must regularly borrow food and supplies. Gale has talked about how people drop by, describing her triumph in baking a chocolate cake in someone's wood stove, and later brownies on their gas burners.

We invested in an international calling card, and when there was service, we could hear her perfectly well. In the few pictures she's posted, she looked delighted, at ease, radiant. In one, she was holding an enormous leaf over her head like an umbrella, which is exactly how she used it when a rain cloud suddenly burst during her travels.

The cutest umbrella I've ever seen.

GALE: email excerpt, May 31, 2014: We in South America have transitioned to the rainy season, and it has truly come in with force.

As a New Englander, I savor and rely on the seasons to help me mark the passage of time. And yet, somehow, I have essentially skipped five of the past six winters, spending them in Peru, Chile, Atlanta, and

Oakland, none of which involved shoveling snow. And now, here I am in Colombia.

The seasonal switch has flipped from summer (defined as humid, though mostly dry) to winter (meaning enough rain to flood every-thing and cause daily debates about whether the river is too high to cross to get into town). While conversations about the weather are as ubiquitous here as in Massachusetts (where winter refers to the friggin' cold time that's filled with snow, hot chocolate, and cuddle puddles by the fire), I've realized that a better way to measure the change in sea-sons is really through what crops are growing.

This is lucky for me, because I like to eat, and I love learning about how everything grows. For example, the season for cacao, the Commu-nity's main export crop, is almost over, because cacao does not like so much water.

It's easy to tell what's in season, because that's whatever we have fall-ing out our ears. People are very kind and bring gifts of a few plantains or several thousand bananas, depending on the season. We haven't run out of fresh beans lately, and the mango trees are tossing their fruits to the ground. We eat those so often that floss has become a permanent fixture in my bag.

When some new-to-us food arrives in our kitchen, we sit there puzzling over it for a minute or two before somebody, small or big, saunters in and casually lays out how to prepare it.

Our kitchen is a mix of hardy *campesino* and delicate Westerner. We don't have a wood stove, as most people here do, but a gas one with two burners. Our *tanque* (water tank), where our water is stored, has a side compartment that we use to wash dishes. We have no refrigerator (after having purchased and broken two in succession, but they now serve nicely as shelves). It can be irritating, but I've found that this setup keeps me connected to my kitchen and the food that I eat, because things don't keep for long. The upside is that the food we eat is always fresh!

We can float things in the tanque to keep them chilled. *Campo* cheese (similar, obviously, to farmers cheese) keeps for about a day, fresh milk for a little over half a day. While we are given or can buy a lot of fresh products, we do make the trek down the mountain about once a week to buy vegetables and other necessities, keeping in mind that whatever we buy, we have to carry up on our backs, and whatever is left over (packaging-wise) must be carried down again or burned.

Gale took a lot of pride in any cake she was able to concoct.

But within these limitations, we in FOR have been undergoing a bit of a kitchen revolution and have managed to make things like cakes on the gas stove. (I was *so* proud.) Any recipe suggestions within the above limitations are welcome!

Because food in general runs the show here, there are plenty of opportunities to get all kinds of advice from people. In this foodie's opinion, learning which crops like what conditions, or which fun gastronomical delights will be making their entrance soon, can be a great social opportunity.

A few years ago, a good friend made a seemingly simple but profound statement about how eating with others is physical sustenance connected to emotional and spiritual sustenance. Ever since, I have been thinking about food and community eating. Here, it is folded into the spin of daily life. The pride people take in growing, harvesting, creating, and sharing food is absolutely one of my favorite ways to connect.

MEG: I flew into Medellín, a large city ringed by mountains. With a full day to myself before Gale arrived to meet me, I had time to walk around the city, enjoying the small shops and the artsy area close to my hotel. People were particularly kind, and in my stop-and-go Spanish, I was able to explain that I was waiting for my daughter. I must have had "innocent traveler" tattooed on my forehead, because a couple of them made a point of telling me not to stay out late by myself and steered me in the direction of my hotel.

Gale and I had time to stroll and find a place for dinner before turning in early for our flight to Cartagena, where we'd chosen to spend a few days. Located in northern Colombia, Cartagena is a port city, with a sixteenth-century walled section and beautiful architecture. Our hotel is located in this labyrinthine quarter, and I was grateful that Gale inherited her sense of direction from Duke and not me.

I was fascinated by all the spiny fruits and wanted to taste every one.

It was a delight to explore the castle outside of town, equipped with the broad-brimmed straw hats (Gale looked adorable in her striped one) with which Colombians protect themselves from the baking heat. We eavesdropped on a guided tour, which felt a teeny bit like cheating, but it was so entertaining that we couldn't help ourselves.

The next day we took a boat to one of the pristine white-sand beaches, where we could explore and then relax on beach chairs set out in front of wooden cabanas. The boat proceeded at a stately pace, giving us and another couple dozen passengers a relaxing half hour to enjoy the breeze. I could not get enough of swimming in the warm waters. Leaving behind the cold and slush of Massachusetts was an unusual treat.

Gale was extremely animated as she talked about her colleagues and how amazing and challenging it could be to communicate with

I don't think we could pass as natives, but it was sure fun to be there.

them. Gale is direct and an exceptional, precise communicator, but she gets riled up when she is not afforded her due. She is passionate about doing the right thing and equally ardent that the messaging be clear.

For my part, I was fascinated to hear about all of it, how the organization works, what their individual and collective roles were, and how the people in the field communicated with those at headquarters in Bogotá.

On the return trip, the boat took off at a startling clip toward shore. Its wake created a huge wave, which rained on a trio standing on deck. Gale and I had noticed them before: a woman (dressed in a colorful silk top, tight pants, and stylish high-heeled sandals) and two casually dressed male companions, all of whom were speaking what sounded like Russian. I was intrigued to see how they would handle this unexpected bath and was impressed when they all laughed, evidently unbothered.

A Cartegena treat: this woman was posing for her friends opposite her,
but we for sure snagged the better photo.

After a leisurely and mostly relaxing three days in Cartagena, we set out for Apartado, to the southwest. A quick flight in a smallish plane was followed by a half-hour ride past mile after mile of banana fields. Gale pointed out the head-swimming number of varieties. Later, I would discover a fondness for the tiny *manzana* bananas (apple bananas) and not just because it's fun to say. The sweet little bites are each just a pop in the mouth.

Our taxi left us off at the station, where we transferred to a jeep that would take us up the mountain to La Holandita, La Unión's sister community, where we planned to spend the night.

GALE: email excerpt, March 13, 2014: The *chivero* is an open-air jeep with storage on the roof and tight seating for eight adults in two facing benches.

To understand what the chivero is like, keep in mind two things. The first is the glee that comes from doing dangerous, transport-related stuff that you can only do in South America. The second is its cartoonish delivery service.

Conjure, if you will, a grassy knoll from which a dirt path spills forth, all animated. The earth is still. Then, from a distance, putt-putt-bing-bang noises grow louder until, all of a sudden, the chivero shoots up over the hill. Suspended for just a wheel-wobbling second before getting sucked back into the earth, it barrels on its way. People stand on the back bumper, swaying to the right and the left with the motion of the vehicle. The cargo piled high on the roof threatens to undermine the vehicle's center of gravity, and bits of paper and debris go flying every which way as it tears down the mountain.

I love the chivero.

MEG: We had enough time to dash to the market for some food to cook that night before our jeep left. We hopped under the roof of the jalopy's open-air back along with a couple of women, two young girls, and a young man. Another man tossed a bag on top and stood on the back fender, holding on to something I couldn't see. We set off and stopped five minutes later. The man hopped off, pulled a few eight-foot-long wooden boards from the side of the street, and put them on the roof. We made a couple more stops and then dropped off the whole load. After a half hour, we were within a block of where we had started.

"This is very unusual," Gale explained, dismayed. "A couple of stops, maybe." We finally headed out of town, making some quick drops, and then came upon a swarm of children. Were they getting out of school at this hour? It was past 6:30 p.m.

Seemingly out of nowhere, a pair of policemen pulled us over. Everyone needed to show ID. We retrieved our passports easily, but others had to fish theirs from bags on the roof. We were sent off within ten minutes, but it had an impact on our mood. There were eyes where we could not see them, assessing us while we bumped down the uneven road. We had been so jolly just moments before, but there was no denying the eerie feeling created by being stopped.

By 6:45 it was completely dark. I remembered from our family trip to Mexico how quickly the transition from light to dark takes place when you're nearer to the equator. None of this lingering light and prolonged goodbyes to the sun at the end of the day. I couldn't see much of the greenery surrounding the potholed, gravelly road. We stopped a few more times, letting off some passengers here, a bag or a message there. Finally, we arrived at La Holandita and jumped down with our backpacks.

A nun dressed in chino pants and a T-shirt greeted us, as did a Bosnian girl and a German girl, both of whom spoke terrific English. They too were staying the night and would travel with us in the morning to La Unión. We made food on the two-burner stove. The Bosnian girl had learned to make *arepas* (flat corn-flour cakes topped with butter or cheese) while living in Venezuela. I was impressed at what could be conjured on those burners.

After feasting and chatting, we turned in for the night under our mosquito netting. I had feared that I would feel claustrophobic, but the netting was light and see-through. Gale slept in the hammock in the main area, preferring the open air to the slightly moldy cast of the mattresses.

Not long after I managed to drift off to sleep, I heard flapping outside my window. Seconds later, a rooster crowed like a cornered animal, setting off an alarming game of telephone. A ripple of roosters sounded around the small community. Then, like a wave, this urgent message restarted with the rooster by my window. A dog responded with a plaintive howl, and this triggered a new call-and-response from the roosters.

Pondering why this was happening at midnight instead of daybreak, I shifted on my super-firm, two-inch-thick mattress and welcomed a bit of shut-eye. An hour later, a nearby cow lowed. This received the same enthusiastic response from the roosters, which clearly could not let any comment go unanswered. Who knew domestic animals were so freaking social?

The next thing I knew, it was 3:05 a.m., and a delicate melody filled the air. In my extreme disorientation I could not place where it was coming from, and after a minute it stopped. Fifteen minutes later the same music-box melody repeated, again with no response from its owner. Or the roosters, thankfully.

When it went off again, I nearly jumped out of bed, ready to find what must be someone's cell phone and throw it in the basin that served as a sink. There was a rustling, the pressing of cell phone buttons, and the bed creaking in the next room. (I learned in the morning that this was one of the girl's reminders to take her medication.)

At 4, the rooster contingent had something else to discuss, and the ringleader outside my window made sure that the community had it clear before settling back down. Close to 5, someone a few houses down the grassy path demonstrated the "one up, everyone up" rule and blared reggae so loudly that I was shocked the roosters had nothing to add.

More surprising to me was that there was no discernible human response. Gale told me much later that the only way to get privacy for intimate moments was to blare music to disguise it. Well now. Once again I learned that part of life is what you're used to. I could fathom nothing more passion-crushing than ear-splitting music, but so be it for my imagination.

By 6:30 we were all awake, making coffee and oatmeal and preparing for our two-hour hike up the mountain to Gale's community. I wondered whether the roosters wanted us to convey any memos to their brethren there. I hoped not. My Spanish was still weak, and I had other plans for my night than deciphering conversations between the community's fowl.

GALE: email excerpt, April 14, 2014: The *campesinos* (farmers) work with their bodies all day, as do we. Like actors, musicians, and dancers, they view taking care of bodies as critical. If you ask somebody here how they are, the response is an immediate and resounding: *mal* (bad). They're going to get through this thing, but it's bringing them down. Like dancers, they embody great everyday capacity and intelligence. It continues to blow me away.

Anybody who doesn't believe that people can be smart with their bodies has obviously never hung out with campesinos, that much is for sure. "It's like skating!" one of them gleefully exclaimed as we made our way down a slick, muddy pass. I watched as he flitted his way down the rocky curves, but I was left agog when I saw him step intentionally onto the side of a rock and slip down it, knowing that he would slide and recover with the next series of steps. And he planned that.

Gale does appreciate her lush environment and how she moves within it.

Their work with tools is done with infinite calculation and alarming precision. My mother compared the setup of felling papayas to pool sharks aiming their next shot: constant, reliable, and (down to the children) impressive. I watched in wonder, remembering that the style of karate I practice was generated by Japanese farmers. This gives me a proud connection with the work they do and a sheepish awe, because I will never be as good with a machete. Their bodies reflect all the pain they have experienced. Everybody shows how incredibly hard they work, because everybody is incredibly strong. That said, the quantities and shapes of their scars are fearsome. Some scars we hear about from other FORistas, and some we can tentatively ask about. But the origin of other scars is best left to the imagination.

MEG: The modernity of Medellín and the touristy section of Cartagena fooled me into thinking that everyday life in rural Colombia would be familiar. On the hike to La Unión, I was struck by the natural beauty of the place as well as the fact that country life in a hot and humid climate will feel different to an American from the Northeast. The hike, although not arduous in terms of technical difficulty, was steadily uphill through rolling and sometimes steep hills. I became winded at times, and Gale reminded me that it was very humid, and that I was carrying fifteen pounds on my back. This felt like small consolation, but we were all dripping when we arrived at her little home.

There was one sink per home, each composed of two parts. Made of concrete, the right-hand side is a large tank filled with water. On the left-hand side was a downward-sloping surface that drains at the bottom. A plastic bowl is used to scoop water for rinsing dishes, teeth, or clothing. It took a little time to get used to, but it was easy enough to splash water on our faces to cool off immediately (until we had the energy for a quick, cold shower). It was also a relief to remove the knee-high mud boots and socks, which felt much too warm now that they weren't necessary.

Hammocks were tucked off to the side of the main room and on the small back porch. The young women who hiked up the mountain with us each climbed into one and fell immediately asleep, giving Gale and me some time to sit on the front porch and gaze at the Community.

GALE: email excerpt, February 15, 2015: Nothing else can slow time and create a glowing, soft moment the way a hammock can. Imagine the most comfortable position you can—and now imagine being suspended and rocking gently in that position. What could be better?

People think that they must feel uncomfortable for a whole night's sleep, but I've found that they are more comfortable than most beds. Napping or dozing in hammocks is just royalty. You can sway yourself to sleep! Swinging in one is something I adore. Hammocks are just the best.

I'm trying out the local form of relaxation. Not sure I could get used to it as a way to sleep through the night, but who knows?

MEG: It was already obvious how much Gale loved it here. She pointed out different dwellings, who lived there, and what she knew about them and their children. It all suited her: engaging with the Community's celebrations and their protests, walking and hiking, learning to cook in new ways and with new foods.

I knew that she was also fed by interactions with others, by the Spanish language, the culture, and the work she was doing. The flush in her face was no longer from the hike. Her deep satisfaction in what she was doing, and her embrace of every aspect of her work was startling and compelling. Although her work was about supporting the Community, keeping them safe, and translating for the military, everyday life goes on—and she relished it.

Her commitment was for a year, but if there was a chance that she could extend it, she likely would. From a distance, I could imagine being impatient for her to get out of this war zone and come home. But being present with her, I couldn't imagine encouraging her to leave.

Gale and I share a love of language. We enjoy a turn of phrase, a double entendre, a malapropism. The nuances of foreign languages—their distinctive sounds, the idiosyncratic phrases, even the misunderstandings—are hard to grasp until you've achieved some level of mastery, and there is no better way to master a language than to be immersed in it. I was just beginning to dream in French when my semester there ended. I was disappointed to have had to leave just as I was on the cusp of fluency.

For her part, after spending time in Argentina, Chile, Costa Rica, and Peru, Gale noticed differences in dialects, accents, meaning, and custom.

I was grateful to be in this lush life with her, and I particularly appreciated that she did not have to rush off for an emergency accompaniment during the week I was there. She and Kaya did spend time every evening writing up observations and being in contact with the people in Bogotá. That was reminder enough that this was not a vacation for her.

GALE: email excerpt, February 15, 2015: Wordplay in English is a strong part of my identity, and I relate it to the music I hear in language.

I still thrill the heck out of myself when I make more complex puns in Spanish, evidence that I am hearing and understanding more masterfully. I can now draw linguistic and social connections that I previously may not have been able to.

Still, anytime I attempt to make a pun, I have to make a thorough check to ensure I actually know what's going on. As exaggerated as my English puns tend to be, they have to be at least double that in Spanish. This works well in demonstrating my awareness that I'm up to something. But sometimes this simply convinces others I'm either a nutbag or far less mature than is appropriate to the situation.

People do seem more inclined to correct my language when I make a less-than-perfect pun than they would if I were speaking more conventionally. Maybe this has more to do with the confidence/cockiness/sureness normally required to pull off a pun, but wordplay is still one of my favorite kinds of puzzles, and I'm not too upset when it fails. (I had an acquaintance who fist-bumped me anytime I made a pun in English, which was just the encouragement I needed and quashed any doubts I might have had. So I'm merrily sallying forth from there.)

MEG: As Gale and I were sitting on the stoop, three little pigs walked by, grazing without once looking up from their work. I wondered how they even landed anything in their mouths, but during my three-day stay they wandered by a number of times, like tiny vegetarian land sharks, ever circulating and eating.

These pigs don't need to build houses. They just roam between them

The horses, cows, dogs, and chickens also roamed freely. Gale and her housemates took advantage of this by tossing banana and papaya peels outside for them to eat. I practiced taking aim with my peel out the six-inch kitchen window to the backyard. Once, a horse obligingly sauntered over to take a banana peel out of our hands, much to my delight.

I had wondered aloud whether I might be able to ride a horse. "Well," Gale had replied. "You'll see." I now understood why it was not easy to explain. The animals roamed free, but that did not mean they were friendly or seeking interaction. In fact, I realized they were unaccustomed to outsiders, unlike on American farms I have visited. Even most of the dogs, while happy to congregate on the porch, did not look for affection except from the people in their homes.

Greeting the locals.

All the skinny animals were, however, happy recipients of whatever food scraps were offered. One cow in particular—a cafe con leche-colored beauty whose tan faded as it moved toward her belly—was particularly forward. Dubbed "Daisy," she had, on more than one occasion, needed to be ushered out of the house. Gale confessed that Daisy had once peed inside. I was appalled, but Gale's roommate calmly reassured me that it wasn't that big a deal: "Really, it mostly drained out right away. We followed it with water immediately, and the cleaning impact was pretty small."

I had to admire Daisy for her perseverance and initiative. Apparently, she had been passing through the house only because she noticed the lemongrass in the backyard garden. On my second day, we learned that Daisy was pregnant, possibly accounting for her headbutting insistence on procuring scraps.

Gale taking an active approach to discussions with Daisy.

I was jolted awake on my first night in La Unión by the sound of grass being ripped from the ground, probably by a horse or cow in search of a midnight snack. The roosters conversed raucously through the night. As I drifted off for perhaps the fourth time, I realized that these entertaining yet aloof creatures were integrated into the community. Within a few days, I was beginning to observe and appreciate their roles. I would have to settle for imitating the calf who bellowed with the intensity of a bull, but in a high-pitched voice.

GALE: email excerpt, October 19, 2014: Pigs are elegant creatures. Whether trotting, ears flapping gaily, and grunting with every fourth bounce, or ambling and mining the land for whatever tasty greens they can find, they do it all on their tippy-toes, achieving a surprising level of charm.

Pigs also love to be scratched, as if they were weird, coarse-haired dogs. This is about the only time they look relaxed. Their buggy eyes tend to look a little neurotic the rest of the time. Pigs are unequivocally my favorite.

On the other hand, hummingbirds are noisy buggers. Part of our job is to be attentive and visible when helicopters fly nearby, but I swear that more than once I sat up, hyperalert, only to see one of those flashy dashers zipping by. Gorgeous creatures, but truly I cannot think of them as elegant any longer.

GALE: Email excerpt, February 15, 2015: Colombia is ravaged by conflict, over fifty years' worth, and everything, in one way or another, revolves around that conflict. The biggest evidence of this is Colombia's central theme of *confianza*, or trust.

Immediately and regularly mentioning confianza as a value shows how tightly knit into the fabric of the culture the concept is. Without confianza, people are definitely selective about what information, opinions, and experiences they share with others (if at all). The idea of having an "instant connection" is rare here, at least in my experience. This isn't to say that people aren't friendly. But the slow reveal of character is just more evident. All relationships (not just romantic) are taken extremely seriously. Confianza is everything, and growing real confianza with people takes a very long time.

In contrast, I come from the northeastern United States, which is about as direct as we get. Beyond that, my family values communicating needs and speaking honestly. I can get antsy and confused if things feel unclear or if something's wrong but nobody's talking about it. So it's been interesting for me to navigate a world that is necessarily more passive-aggressive than I am used to or comfortable with.

In some ways, this is painful for me, because I believe so much in direct communication. But people *are* talking directly, just in a different way. It's like a code that people recognize, and they understand why lying/fibbing might sometimes be better. I'm still working a lot of it out.

I tend to live my life as a pretty open book, both because I like feeling honest and because I tend to get exhausted otherwise. But this year, I have learned to live somewhat vaguely and in a rather arranged way, at least with strangers.

This is a safety precaution that we are trained for. Right off the bat, we say we work "with an NGO." If pushed, we add "that works with displaced populations" rather than dropping "HUMAN RIGHTS."

All this makes me think a lot about secrets, their place and necessity. Is it worth having secrets? Do we need secrets? From whom? Prior to this year, I would have said that people keep secrets or lie perhaps because they are ashamed or because the truth reveals an uglier side than they are willing to expose. But now I know people whose secrecy has literally kept them alive. I know people who didn't have someone in whom to place their trust, when the consequences of telling the truth could literally be the cost of life. That's hard for me to swallow.

So are secrets good? Are they a healthy part of having a private life versus a public life? If I had more secrets, would I be forced to activate a more present inner life? Would my abilities to work things out on my own strengthen or expand?

As foreigners, it's more difficult to be believed when things do go wrong, because we're less in the know and therefore skilled in backpedaling or defending ourselves. Still, especially as time goes on, I am learning to become more aware and more sensitive to what certain silences mean, when people are hiding things and want me to know them, and when they're hiding things and *don't* want me to know.

For my part, I'm learning to show when I need people to be aware that I can see through them, for better or worse. Who trusts first? What are the changing roles of changing authorities here? I think a lot about truth and confianza and what integrity means and where its meaning has become irreparable in this country.

Living here can thus be emotionally costly. Every once in a while, the pain and distrust hits you pretty hard. People often ask foreigners what we're doing here, and having to carefully navigate that conversation sometimes feels like subsisting on food that might make a mess at any moment—like a burrito that you're always worried will leak no matter how carefully you've folded it.

You can tell when people are giving you sideways answers, or don't want to answer your question at all, after a while. And you start to create theories about why they might not answer you, whether for reasons of security or discomfort. It's pretty wild to consider that the whole country uses this sort of survival-mode practice, and it's been tricky working and living where suspicion is the baseline, however necessary.

MEG: "I will need to take you to every house in the village!" Gale declared. That had sounded reasonable but undoable even before we arrived. It was not like the end of a soccer game line, with its hand-slapping "good game, good game, good game." Each meeting would be personal. Certainly there wouldn't be time to fit this into my three-day visit.

The second day, we headed up the hill to a farm. Gale peered through the tiny window into the dimly lit interior, calling, "¿*Alo*?" Marielena greeted us and welcomed us inside the gate.

She was grinding corn in a waist-high pestle to feed a donkey. "He is not eating. See how swollen he is here?" She firmly punched the animal's lower neck, for some reason. "This is not good," she said, clearly worried. I marveled at her ability to read the animal's health.

We walked through a densely grown yard filled with low bushes, flowers, and equipment, and into a small kitchen area with a very low ceiling and a wood-burning stove.

She shooed two tiny cats off an upturned log that made a bench and offered us seats as she retrieved some wood to stoke the fire. The hard-packed dirt floor was swept clean. Marielena pointed to a small side table with a shelf underneath. "See the duck and the chicken asleep there?" Charmed, I had not even noticed them cuddled together.

She took eggs and busied herself by the stove as we chatted. How did I like it here? What were we doing? Where was my husband? I labored through my responses, using my high school Spanish. Gale interrupted only when I answered in French, which, frustratingly, was more accessible than my Spanish. As if by magic, Marielena turned, holding two bowls of soup made with what looked like oversize kidney beans, chunks of banana, with a cooked egg on top. I was not expecting a meal. "¡*Ay, muchas, muchas gracias!*" I exclaimed before eagerly tucking into it.

Marielena looked me directly in the eye, her manner and tone conveying absolute conviction. "You do us great honor by visiting us here."

The tears that sprang up instantly hindered my ability to form words. "Oh, Marielena. The honor is mine. Thank you so much. You are so very generous." I was stammering, searching for the right words, and felt deeply humbled.

She handed us chunks of bread, which stymied my attempts at formulating more coherent thoughts. "*Gracias, otra vez gracias*" (Thank you, again, thank you) was as eloquent as I could manage.

Perhaps I was being presumptuous, but even with a great deal unspoken, I felt that she was telling me that she appreciated the work my daughter was doing in the village and also that I had traveled to visit. She felt my respect for her, for what she was doing. She had chosen this life very deliberately. This is no casual community, and their very lives depended on the work that is done there, and in their connection to one another.

As we prepared to leave, Marielena asked when I was going to return. I had not even entertained this notion, but I was now wondering the same thing. She was not asking out of politeness. She truly wanted to know. I could only tell her that I had no plans at the moment, but I knew that if and when I returned, I would have a friend to welcome me.

GALE: email excerpt, May 31, 2014: It has been thundering and lightning almost daily lately—sometimes all at once, but more often a single order of each. Every once in a while, there will be a tour of thunder, but more frequently we see single strips of lightning illuminating the sky and retreating in the same breath, with no rain or thunder in sight. Among all the heavy downpours, it makes for a delicate streak of beauty and danger laced against the mountain range.

I consider the contrast. The serenity of the landscape belies the intensity of the divide.

GALE: Email excerpt, February 15, 2015: Colombian fashion is notable in a few distinct categories.

There are no "crazy leggings" in Colombia, because all of the leggings are crazy! Considered just short of professional, leggings are usually brightly colored and patterned, and lots of people wear them. The big separation is: "I am from Bogotá, I wear only black. I am a city slicker and will occasionally wear a little color or an animal pattern" versus everybody else (especially in warmer locations) wearing brightly colored, beachy clothing. But clothing is form-fitting everywhere.

Colombians are big on hats, which come in different shapes based on region, although they are all awesome. New York Yankees baseball caps are ubiquitous. I theorize that this has to do with the sexy design of the logo, as opposed to a recruitment or takeover plot. As a New Englander, I should be offended on principle, but I mostly think it's funny.

My favorite hat was spotted in one of the places we accompany. We were on the coast and had seen these awesome baseball caps with tall, mirrored letters on the front. The first one I saw was red with shiny gold letters that read "BOSS" (do not be surprised if I return to the US with one of those), or possibly "PUMA" or "KING." But the hat we saw came walking in on an eight-year-old who was casually dropping by with his family to buy a chicken for dinner. He sweetly greeted everybody, which was when we saw the unassuming flash of his hat reading, "FUCK." Brilliant. Kept us entertained, perplexed, and somewhat embarrassed for hours.

Hair for women must be as long as you can grow it (mine is longer than it's been in seven or eight years, and I swear that's only about half laziness). Men get creative, super-cool shapes shaved into their hair (*motilado*, for those interested). Mohawks and fauxhawks are common. Casual making-it-up on my part would assume this has to do with getting hair off one's skin to combat the humidity, but I haven't asked anybody about it.

Colombians only rarely get gray hair, and if they do, it's later in their life. They have very little body hair in general, which is a topic of endless conversation and entertainment. The campesinos ask us, rather frankly, if we think body hair is beautiful or what. I swear my own forearm hair turned a softer, golden color when I was in the Community. Full beards are not common here. It was a total hoot when my tall, pale, red-headed colleague shaved his four-inch beard and returned to the Community. More than one Community member thought he was a different person.

Nails are paramount. On women, long nails are valued, as they can be turned into tiny wearable art-lets. Ring fingers and pointer toes are painted distinctively and might have some lil jewels on them. Colombian men are generally expected to have nice nails. Even in high-up military and government meetings, men's hands are always well groomed, sometimes buffed and polished with a clear nail lacquer.

In the countryside men's manicures are less common, but a long thumbnail is considered extremely beautiful—and maybe valuable. "They have many uses," claimed one campesino as he disconcertingly clicked his nail between his two front teeth. When I professed confusion, he demonstrated how he could avoid handling something gross by picking up a shirt with his nails rather than his hands. "Aha," I said.

MEG: Some neighbors determined that the papayas that dwell high in the tall trees of Gale and Kaya's yard were ready to deliver their fleshy goodness. One of them fashioned a tool out of a machete lashed to a very long pole. He retrieved a tarp from their house, where it was stored specifically to catch the plummeting papayas when they are harvested.

Gale and Kaya held the tarp, stretched wide, under one of the trees. Like a pool shark taking aim, he carefully positioned them until he was satisfied with their placement. Papayas are large, and getting hit with one from a distance of thirty feet could result in a serious injury, to say nothing of the waste of a papaya. With a well-practiced thwack, he swung the long pole, freeing the first papaya from its tether. It came hurtling down, landing with a thunk in the center of the tarp. Satisfied, he examined it and then set it aside. The process repeated as he surveyed the direction each fruit leaned and how it was fastened, before moving Gale and Kaya first left, then right, then back just a bit. Again, he took aim and chopped the papaya stalk, sending his quarry directly

I would need a much larger target for the papaya.

into the waiting cloth below. I was mesmerized by this game and by his knowledge.

I was eager to try out the spoils of their labor, but no, he admonished, this one needed another day before it would be perfect for consumption. Fortunately, the first one was ready to eat. On their own, papayas are quite bland. But add a bit of fresh lime juice, as Kaya declared necessary, and they are transformed into a tasty, tangy, juicy treat. I completely agreed with this assessment. Rarely have I experienced a transformation of a food from something I would never choose to eat into one that I could not resist.

I had had a similar experience when visiting our friends, Pete and Sharon, who had built a house in Honduras. At a friend's farm, we tasted a starfruit, which was quite sour. Later he gave us a miracle berry (*Synsepalum dulcifucum*), and everything we ate after that tasted sweet, including the starfruit. Even a few hours later, I took a sip of black coffee and found that even that had a sweet taste.

GALE: email excerpt, February 15, 2015: We on the Bogotá team generally do a minimum of three to four accompaniments per month in three to five distinct locations. Ideally, we'd know about our accompaniments well ahead of time and could therefore purchase cheap plane tickets. But this is not ideal. As we say, this is "the very human world of human rights," meaning, among other things, super volatile schedule-wise. And so we need the cheapness and flexibility that buses allow.

Because fewer people have cars here, they travel everywhere by bus. Given that bus travel is a huge part of the Latin American experience, and considering how much we travel, I believe myself to be somewhat of an authority on them.

The buses we ride on long trips are large coaches with cushy seats (think Greyhound). In contrast, the smaller buses that go shorter distances hurtle around, defying the laws of physics, and terrify even the boldest of souls.

I thought people were kidding/ridiculous when they asked me if I had a jacket, or at least a long-sleeved shirt to bring just for the ride. But seriously, the air conditioning is Arctic-level. Bring your blankets and socks. Of course, it's preferable to the heat, especially for a ride so long.

Whenever we make a stop, food vendors surge forward, which is so fun. They board the bus yelling, "Empanada-empanada-empanada" (empanadas are small, thin breads filled with meat and onion, or cheese, then deep fried) or "Mango-mango-mango-mango-mango" (mangos are simply delicious).

On long rides, the bus sometimes stops at inconvenient times, but the food then is often really tasty! My favorites are the 2 a.m. stops, when everybody stumbles off the bus to do zombie walks and order rib soup.

Regardless of the timing, the message is: "delicious-fried-things-WAKE-UP-AND-SMELL-THE-COFFEE-this-will-make-you-feel-like-a-gross-greasy-human-later-ya-sucker-but-IT-IS-SO-DELICIOUS-YOU-BETTER-TRY-IT-NOW-CHEAP-CHEAP-MORNING-CHEAP-CHEAP-CHEAP."

Despite the time involved, I don't mind the buses. I enjoy having the time to talk about deep or time-consuming things with my colleagues, discover fun snacks, and compare regional foods. The seats are pretty good for sitting and sleeping (except for that one time when my seat hurled me forward every time we went over a bump. That was a long night).

I will never again pull a rookie move and forget toilet paper, because bathroom creativity is not fun creativity. I have mastered the part where you walk back to the microscopic restroom. I laugh like hell, but silently, while getting thrown back and forth by the movement of the bus. It is surely the most preposterous trek to pee ever. Nobody else seems to think this is funny, and I don't know why.

Depending on the time of day and the length of the ride, they might play anywhere from two to four movies. I've now seen *Blended* (a comedy!) five times. The three Christian-themed movies I've seen were somewhat interesting and inoffensive. Highlights included two dance movies and a couple others I would actually watch on my own. One awesome ride included an amalgamation of all of the *Lord of the Rings* movies, five and a half hours or so. This was so hilarious and bizarre—like a weird bus fever dream—that I didn't even care that it was on until 3:30 in the morning. (10:30, exhausted, sleep, wake up, "Oh, Smaug! Nice," sleep, wake up, 12:30, "Battle of the Ents, right on," 2:30, "Ugh, Shelob is so crazy," 3:00, "Frodo, just THROW IT IN already!") Dubbing, while odd, does allow me to practice reading lips and learning some of the more off-the-wall phrases in Spanish.

But the majority are horrendously violent films scraped from the sludge of the movie sewage pit. I have learned to recognize these abominations early: I now pay attention to the names of production companies, and the opening music tells you whether it's acceptable or crusher in about two and a half bars. They play these movies at an absolutely appalling volume that no MP3 player can drown out. If you try to look out the window instead of watching, your reflection is there, mocking you (there are curtains only on the better buses).

This class of movie is big on things squishing, dripping, or breathing jaggedly, so looking away from Halle Berry almost-crying for three hours or Liam Neeson questioning some sort of mafia agent is even more anxiety-producing than just watching the damn thing. The plots are unbendingly characterized by a macho man spurred into revenge mode due to the menacing/murder of his lady partner and/or daughter.

In my most bitter late-night/early-morning rages, I say that these movies show a solid representation of the Colombian agenda. I try not to say that the rest of the time, because that's a terrible overgeneralization. But when I am feeling embittered, it is hard.

Although much time is spent on buses or hiking, not all the trips are by land.

MEG: La Unión consists of a cluster of buildings—single-story homes arranged into three rows—including a school and a preschool/child care. The trip to the city of Apartado to find supermarkets, clothing stores, or a reliable internet cafe requires the ninety-minute hike, followed by the open-air jeep ride. The men rise early and head to the farms, stopping on the way at the home of Marielena to buy her arepas and lunches to take with them. Because there is little variation in the time the sun rises and sets, the routine continues year-round, as does the production of crops, even if the type of crop varies.

The people in the community may wear clothing that is torn, or stained, or is covered in foreign words or the logos of American companies. The patterns do not matter. If it is serviceable, it can be worn.

The children are bundles of effervescent energy, bounding with curiosity and openness, beauty and ebullience. Their innocent understanding of their situation is a balm, a necessary and healing additive. This is what they know. They are at home, comfortable and easygoing in the safety of a community with no threat of cars, no danger from motorcycles or gangs. They can be completely themselves, utterly able to live in the moment, and with each other. Contrast this with the adults' experience and knowledge of the military, guerrillas, and paramilitary, and with their everyday attention to news small and large.

There are any number of similar communities; what sets this village apart is its declaration of peace. They have come together to farm their land, without supporting the military, paramilitary, or guerrillas.

This sounds straightforward, but it is not. Any of those groups might perceive this stance as a threat and react accordingly, which

The kids are welcoming, and everyone enjoys this kind of accompaniment.

could mean anything from occupying land, to eating or destroying crops, to, in some cases, rounding up leaders and shooting them. Such was the devastation experienced by the Community in 2005, four years after its formation. Presumably, the assumption was that the Community would perish once its leaders were violently removed. With the aid of FOR, the village is no longer invisible and has in fact been transformed into a beacon of possibility. I see the people of this Community as heroes. I admire their conviction, their clear priorities, and the intentionality of their lives.

For its part, FOR/Peace Presence seeks to maintain neutrality as well. While they are clearly here as a form of protection, they are not bodyguards, nor are they attempting to control or sway the Community's decisions in any way (think *Star Trek*'s prime directive of noninterference as much as possible). At the same time, they inevitably

There is not a way to peace. Peace is the way.

develop relationships while still maintaining their roles as witnesses and accompaniers. They cannot favor particular Community members, but it is only natural that close bonds will form.

Getting to know and trust one another is important anywhere, but particularly here, in a community with a population of about a couple hundred people in total. The more they (the FORistas) are considered a part of the Community, the less it might feel like being watched or watched over, both of which necessitate some distance in the relationship. Though one might wonder whether there may at times be some resentment, this does not appear to be the prevailing reaction. Without FOR/Peace Presence in their village, they remain at risk.

GALE: email excerpt, October 28, 2015: I've discovered that some experiences and skills have become almost miraculously well developed. For example, I now have a good sense of what time it is based on the position of the sun. In Colombia, being so close to the Equator, the sun surges like a rocket at dawn and plunges at dusk, almost exactly 6–6.

There are also defined dry and wet seasons, with only minor variations in heat, and more in humidity. As a New Englander, I find this extremely odd. I am unconditionally affectionate about the nutso oscillating weather, with its characteristic changes of season. Given my background, I had to ask my friends and *acompañadxs*, in order to understand it. While I couldn't pin down an exact answer, it was real fun to think about!

I'm also better at thinking through logistics now, and I have a sharper sense of the difference in how I come across to others versus how I'm feeling internally. And I know more about land and nature now! This one's a major plus: learning to spot tasty fruits is beneficial to body and mind.

On the flip side, I've become acquainted with a host of new physical experiences, not all of them nice. Those of you who have spent more than 2.5 or so seconds with me know that I have the sweetest blood known to any mosquito. If you know me slightly better, you also know that bites itch like hell and I'm incapable of leaving them alone. At home, this means that I have some semi-banged-up-looking legs for a few weeks in the summer. But here, my skin is at the mercy of whatever the rainforest inexplicably hurls at it. Mosquitoes suck. My face is invariably slick with oil (although I wash it a lot). Even something as minor as a papercut never seems to heal.

In January, my first round of bites became so bad that I had to get various topical creams to apply. That was annoying, but more recently, my many swollen bites crossed the line. I assure you that none of them hurt, and I was treating them with Band-Aids—but not for too long, because fungus can start to grow if you leave them on for more than a day. You know it's just too much when you can't have a conversation about anything else.

Oh, and one of my fingertips doubled in size, filling with pus and pain! Only after 104 pills (not exaggerating, I hated that week real bad) was I able to have normal conversations again. The one party favor I get from this month of pure eeeeeeegh is that the nail on the afore-mentioned finger has made its excuses and slowly edged away. Funny moments include catching a grain of rice underneath the nail and problem-solving for excavation. It'll be good soon.

MEG: I was largely reassured once I returned from my trip. It is not that I felt that there were no risks. There were plenty, and I learned months and even years later that some other FORistas encountered much more difficulty than Gale and Kaya did during their stint there. (Read: They were present when shots were fired.)

It is more than a little ironic that this is the stretch of time when Gale has withheld the most information about what she is seeing and doing. This was true in some of her later accompaniments. Perhaps it was more tolerable because it was closer to the end, and I hoped that she would fill us in soon. I learned long afterward that the accompa-niers deliberately left out many details about their work, assuming that their phones were tapped. It is unbearable to think about the kinds of atrocities she was learning about (or witnessing?). It is not OK at any age, but what twenty-three-year-old is capable of facing the knowledge of such stunning (and recent) violence?

I respect her decisions, as an adult, both to take the job and to make sure that she had what she needed (in every way) while performing it. But I was devastated that she was exposed to humans who harm other humans.

I know that her job affords her a way to separate herself from the pain of others. She must maintain a kind of distance in order to ask the kinds of questions she must ask, so that she can work effectively. Just as a reporter needs to walk the line between being too drawn in and too far removed, and a therapist needs to balance connection with a safe distance, so must Gale navigate offering the right level of empathy.

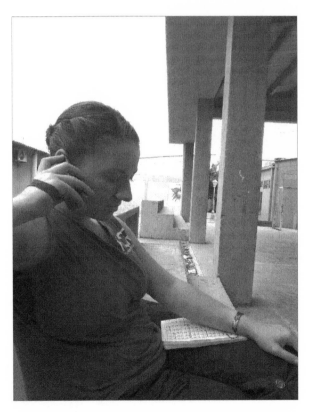

While I was there, I did not often see the evidence of Gale checking in with headquarters, but it was clearly happening on a regular basis.

She knew there would be times when she would come up against unthinkable cruelty. There is a difference between the abstract knowledge of atrocities and the reality of knowing people who have lost relatives or limbs or dignity or a place to live, however long ago. I don't know how much FOR can do about dealing with secondary trauma. I know I can't protect her from it. With that in mind, going to visit Gale was absolutely essential for me. I needed to have a realistic gauge for what she was dealing with, at least as much as I could.

Parents cannot eliminate risk. We can shore up our children so that when they encounter it they can make choices from a conscious, deliberate place. And we can fervently hope that when they encounter the inevitable difficulties that life serves up, randomly and unpredictably, that they will have the resilience to weather the storm and know where to find the support to get them through.

GALE: email excerpt, October 19, 2014: I remember one time accompanying in a cacao field, hearing gunfire a little ways away, and thinking *That was the sound of someone dying.* And it was true. We learned later that one guerrilla and one soldier were killed that day.

Before coming here, I thought military decisions were made in closed rooms or hidden huts, with the orders being executed digitally—or somehow more cleanly, despite knowledge to the contrary.

But no. People scale the ground, they make plans, and then groups of individuals work to realize them against other individuals. In our case, that means they walk around the same mountains we do, experience the same jungles, heat, bugs—and utter fear. No matter what armed group they are part of, many of them were recruited when they were minors. We often walk past soldiers, and there is not one time when I don't notice how young they look. When I look into the eyes of the uniformed men—often plucked from their native regions in order to serve elsewhere (a common military strategy designed to disconnect the soldiers from the surrounding populations)—more often than not I see uncertainty and fear. Dressed identically, they are all so different. The petrified young soldiers shoot at other young men, who are also shooting and similarly petrified.

Then we hear about it later, maybe from people who have heard from someone else, or maybe from the military on the radio letting us all know how many guerrillas (meaning people) have been "neutralized."

And then I visit my neighbors. And I cannot understand how this is the same country where people who are so incredibly generous and loving are living alongside a very real, nasty war.

GALE: Email excerpt, October 9, 2014: My body is different. After walking so many trails—some of it damn fast—my balance, which started out good, is now excellent. I can handle humidity better. I never want to see a bug again, and so help the next sorry suckers that set their sights on me. The scars will fade eventually. And I can sleep in a hammock now. I love that.

My heart is different. I understand strongly that everybody has their own things going on. I am both quieted into reflection of my own upsets and humbled by the trust in connection and desire for understanding. I have been reminded by my teammates how many different ways there are to connect with people and to look for the gems that people inevitably have to offer. Above all, unexpected opportunities arise from conversations that divert from the topic at hand. As I've said before, sometimes impulsiveness is just the thing.

My mind is different. I have learned what strategy looks like, on a conflict level, on a community level, on a team level, and on an interpersonal level. I think more efficiently and am better able to figure out what I and my team want and need. I'm getting better at improvising. When I make Spanish puns now, people don't think I'm nuts. My mom has begun calling me Flex, because my improved flexibility continues to floor those who know me well.

MEG: When she was only six or seven, Gale would answer the phone and announce to callers that I worked late on Mondays, Wednesdays, and Thursdays, and that I would be home at 9. In school, instructions were critical for Gale, and their clarity crucial. It would drive her around the bend to have teachers change deadlines or expectations without notice or very good reason. She could work with many different kinds of parameters, but it was not easy for her to mix them up or suddenly decide on an alternative.

This is not to say that Gale is not creative or spontaneous. In fact, she is exceptionally creative, as evidenced by the way she dances. From jewelry to pottery to knitting, every craft she does with her hands turns to beauty. Gale is also creative in the way she lives her life and thinks about things. She was part of a group that participated in Destination Imagination (originally called Odyssey of the Mind) for most of her childhood. The kids in each group would be given a challenge, which they would solve by making a skit with costumes, scenery, dialogue, and equipment they would create. Her team went twice to the global finals.

But rules have always been important to her. Kate and I will pause and look both ways before crossing the street, but Duke and Gale wait at the crosswalk until the little figure is green before they step off the curb.

Colombia, I knew, demanded changes quickly and with conviction. This was vital for safety, and for something as practical as a shift in the weather. But I realized that flexibility became part of her while she was there.

GALE: *Reflections on returning home:* This work was highly collaborative. The organization as a whole, Fellowship of Reconciliation Peace Presence (FORPP), had a team of six to seven while I was there, including one director, two supervisory and urban traveling team members in Bogotá, and three members in the countryside.

Accompaniment is a pressure cooker; people's security is on the line, and you have to constantly monitor what you say so as not to breach security or come off as giving people directives or opinions, which is prohibited. Among other things, you have to keep your cool, remember the news you hear to share with the team, strike exactly the right tone when meeting with authorities and accompaniment partners, and (depending on the situation) keep your fellow accompanier in sight at all times. Plus, FORPP operates on a consensus model, meaning everybody must be in agreement about any movement the team makes. The teams also change people around for one reason or another once every two or three months.

As such, the relationships among your team are absolutely vital. Communication, patience, and trust are the most important qualities, and you learn a lot in a hurry about how everyone operates.

I gained so much from my fellow accompaniers that I extended my contract another six months (beyond the initial twelve) in order to soak in all that I could. I was lit up by witnessing their brilliance in talking with the people we accompanied, their analysis, their dedication, their playfulness, and their passion. I could not have been more lucky in the shining pillars of humans I have been able to travel, laugh, and learn with.

The teammate I connected with the most was Kaya. Kaya's warm caramel skin and understanding dark eyes made Colombians ask if she was Latina. She's not, but people didn't always believe her, because she felt so comfortable to them, as she does to everybody.

Kaya is magnetic, and this made her exceptional at the relational part of our job, where we learned by talking to people. We think similarly enough that we understood each other smoothly, and we shared an implicit trust in each other's approach that made it feel easy, even when it wasn't.

I called her Snow White because children and animals loved to visit our house. We were well matched in many ways. Our birthdays are April 3 and 4 of the same year, so we got to reflect on and celebrate our growth together. Making and sharing a meal always felt exciting, because of our mutual enthusiasm for flavor and freshness, no matter the occasion or lack thereof. A humble salad became a meal, perfectly done eggs were always savored, and fresh beans and rice became the ambrosia of these mountains.

We loved to sing, and more than once our chores took on a spontaneously Disney-esque hue. One of us would be quietly humming, the other would harmonize, we would sing as much as we knew, then revert to our tasks. It got even better once we decided to learn songs together, which we recorded and sent to our families for the holidays. We both faced challenging situations back at home and helped each other by listening, reminding the other to be gentle with ourselves, and dancing.

I am so proud to have shared so much space with Kaya. We were a dream team. If it sounds like I'm a little in love with her, that's because I am. If you met her, you would be too.

Buddies.

When people ask me how my experience in Colombia compares to that in other destinations, I answer by reflecting on what I want to keep with me now that I'm home.

The biggest one is absolutely Colombia's food culture, which is notable for being fresh, if not enormously varied. I became attached to the quality, variety, and abundance of fruit. I was dazzled—and spoiled, really—by the array. I tried them all, with total disregard for which ones are considered appropriate for eating versus which were for juice only, you loon.

People from all walks of life say, "We're all campesinos." It's odd that there is so much stigma and scorn against the campesino community farmers within Colombia, when the culture is prevalent even beyond the countryside. It's a beautiful way of life that seeps into larger society in various ways. The standard Colombian wakeup time seems remarkably early (6:30 is average, and things are moving by 7:30 at the latest). Around 6:30 p.m., once it's getting dark outside, everything slows down, and it's soon time to settle down and go to bed, sooo early.

People would traditionally stop their machete work and eat lunch, or come down from the mountain for a little while to eat. It is a Big Damn Deal, and is effectively a day-stopper. If you happen to mention that you haven't had lunch, you may be met with looks of horror followed by relieved understanding when you say you're going to find something to eat. As an accompanier, you better hope that no emergencies or significant events occur between noon and 2 p.m. If you are lucky enough to get military officials on the phone in that time span, they more than likely will thank you for the call, but they're eating lunch right now and could you call back in an hour or so? On the other side, the people we would accompany, although usually rushing around, would still stop at some point to eat a substantial meal before moving on to the next location. It was comforting to have something to depend on, especially when it was so delicious.

Virtually everything stops on Sundays. Many people also take Saturdays off, but Colombians often work multiple jobs to make ends meet, and so having more than one day allocated to rest is not a given.

In general, the idea of allotted time for rest feels wise and necessary. This stubborn adherence to breaks is good, because it means people actually take them.

I am attached to the culture of dance and movement in Colombia. A Latino friend recently rejected the stereotype of the loud, effusive, salsa-dancing continent as a vast oversimplification. I had to agree, but Colombians are actually incredible dancers—and movers in general—managing and working their bodies with ease. Movement flows throughout everyday life.

I've been to other places in Latin America, and truly Colombia dances. The accessibility of dance classes is widespread and very reasonably priced. Without fail, I noticed people who came into the classes as drop-ins and were just jaw-droppingly good. Colombians are open with beginners and are thrilled with any learning we do. And this nation's kids can shake and pop a booty with unmatched rawness and finesse. People do just dance in the street in some places. I am attached to the notion that bodies are natural, and they are beautiful, and anybody trying to move can do so—as proven by the simple fact that they already are.

The distinction between inside and outside is fluid. Maybe it's due to the heat or the lack of building supplies, but in the *campo* it's common for kitchens to be partially or completely exposed. It's also common for the largest living area to be a covered outdoor space, where people can drift in and out and sit—especially in the hammocks (my fave) hung there—and gather as they like. I love the fluidity of a community where it's normal for the people you most adore to feel free to just come over and hang out. The lack of physical barriers between inside versus outside may be related to the love of nature. Appreciation of, and pride in, the beauty of the country is universal.

In terms of other people, I found it impossible to do this kind of work without immersing myself in a sort of platonic, or professional, love. Sitting with people, sometimes chatting, but often in total silence, is a specific, focused emotional space.

I'm a little shy when first meeting people. It was comfortable to get to know them by being with them and seeing how they move in space, and how they treat their families, other accompaniers, and me. It was literally my job to get to know people as respectfully and deeply as possible, swiftly and in ways that allowed them to feel able to share about their lives. I learned to find what's interesting and potentially stirring about everybody.

A mixed aspect of Latin American life are the *piropos* (catcalls), which come in varying degrees of creativity and intensity. I'm not a fan. I don't like walking down the street as if I exist for the affirmation of my attractiveness. I particularly don't like that catcalls usually have more to do with the ego of the caller than dazzling the call-ee. The worst are what I call "hungry eyes," when the gaze of a perfect stranger seems to indicate that they want to consume you—in a predatory, violent way, not a sexy one. In some cases, the stare comes complete with a full turning of the head, murmuring things that you can't hear and never want to, and the raw understanding that you are being appraised for your value as meat.

But it's impossible for me to stay angry with something so constant, so I take it instead to mean that I should never feel sensitive about my appearance again! I've always got a hot bod somewhere in Latin America.

To help you all follow the nuances, I have made the following Official Ranking of Piropos! The most popular ones are (from worst to best):

6/7. *Mi reina/princesa* ("my queen/princess"): I hate these, because the sense of servitude makes me wildly uncomfortable. The meaning changes when straight women in shops say it, but that makes it almost worse.

5. *Hermosa* ("pretty"): This one pretty much means nothing, because it just acknowledges that I'm somewhere on the attractiveness scale—which is duh based on being a woman who exists and walks around in the world sometimes—so, honestly, it's kind of a gimme.

4. *Nena* ("baby"): This is cute and makes me feel fun. It's less fun when it happens in official contexts, which reminded me how young and female I am, rather than how seriously they should be taking me. I like it when women call me *nena*, because it feels like a female solidarity thing.

3. *Mami*: I know I probably shouldn't like this one, as it's questionable in terms of feminist values, but I really do. Makes me feel attractive. I can still be a feminist because I'm choosing it, but I'm aware I don't need to be a hot mother in order to be attractive.

2. *Guapa*: I *love* this one. Guapa in most countries refers to a cute/handsome attractiveness, but Colombians use it for when you are strong. Often accompanied by an appreciative look, it's similar to "babe," which I use for those who are strong and work hard. Sexy.

1. *Doctora* ("doctor"): Used for those you respect. I don't always feel deserving of the title (considering I'm not in med school or graduate school [yet?]).

BONUS! The Biggest Head Scratcher Award goes to "¡Here come the Niña, the Pinta, and the Santa María!" What? Like, for conquering? What?

In the end, I can live without piropos.

It would be hard for me to live in Colombia because of its militarization. The army is everywhere, which I never got used to, even though I talked to these guys all the time. I have no way of proving it, but I have to wonder if it does things to the public trust when the military is ubiquitous. It even affects everyday language: Colombia's "You're welcome" is "*a la orden*," meaning "To the (military) command." It's weird to feel like you're giving orders when you ask for a sweet bread or a coffee.

But Colombian Spanish is beautiful. The language in Bogotá is some of the most standard that Spanish can get, which makes it easy to understand. I don't sound like a native speaker, but my language skills do confuse people about my origin. Of course there are moments when I just don't get what's going on, or I've lost a thread, but these moments are so much fewer and farther between.

Spanish has shades for everything. There are multiple forms of the past and future, and lovely, yet still mundane, ways to present things in the now. I am learning how to add definitiveness to some things and apply acceptable uncertainty to others. They are, at this point, a cross between educated guesses and calculated experiments. I like fiddling with the linguistic implications on social movements and change, and tracking and checking my guesses from one country to another.

There are so many different things to do when accompanying that it is virtually impossible to find the job boring. Getting physically, emotionally, and politically ready for accompaniments, finding our way and getting the right buses, figuring out how to talk to people, filling in the gaps between what we know bureaucratically and what has happened recently, making process-based predictions, figuring out where we fit into the larger picture, preparing for and navigating meetings with *acompañadxs,* other accompaniment organizations, various police and military officials, ministers, ambassadors, UN, and others—these were all things we did. I did.

Other than talking with acompañadxs, my favorite part about the office work of accompaniment was the amazing conversations with my babely colleagues. Which part of this situation are we actually accompanying? Is our accompaniment effective? Which things worked from our last accompaniment, and which things should we change this time? What should we be publishing and communicating? Where should we apply pressure? Most importantly, where are all of our team members right now, and how do we coax and cajole our schedule into cooperation?

As a bit of a technophobe, I somewhat cartoonishly tried to avoid team social media production. Learning the political and social histories and contexts of multiple acompañadxs was really challenging for me.

In a related vein, one of the aspects of accompaniment that people say is hard is the principle of non-inherency, meaning not opining on the personal or political processes of acompañadxs, to them or anybody else. This was easy in the beginning: I knew my role. Non-inherency made me feel able to do the work, standing as witness and in solidarity with those being marginalized, and stepping to the side to allow their informed-through-experience, personally-affected voices to be the louder ones. Our acompañadxs were also extremely capable people overall.

As time went on, though, the issue became more real to me. As I learned more and became more passionate about the rights and struggles of our acompañadxs, it became harder to maintain that boundary.

As an *acompañante*, we are most valuable for our foreignness, which is also a privilege: We have the choice to leave, and we understand we're not leaving our home in doing so. Accompaniers by definition have the ability to create bigger spaces for nationals to act, and accompaniers can leave. Our position of living consistently in the Peace Community is a very different, extremely isolated circumstance. But even there, we left.

Being outsiders was tricky to navigate. As a young, white, short, stocky, bug-attracting woman with a background in human rights, and being from the United States, I felt that every part of me was called out at some point in contribution to or working against the work we were doing. As I continued to know and admire acompañadxs, it became harder not to advise on processes. The temptation to share as friends rather than colleagues became stronger and was one indicator of it being time to leave.

A simultaneously empowering, relieving, existential, and stinging reality was that we did represent an organization. While we were from different countries, our overall nationality was "not here." We were replaceable in our positions. It was interesting to know both how vital and nothing we were.

Finally, there was the question of how much secondary, and occasionally primary, trauma one can take and stay healthy. I happen to be a somewhat sensitive person, but I wasn't entirely aware of how much it was affecting me until I left. I'm still figuring some degrees of that out. No amount of preparation or reflection would necessarily be helpful. It was often the smallest things that planted the worst thoughts, like invisible splinters that the most patient of tweezers could not swiftly remove.

After a year and a half, I was simply done. To end on a high note, beyond the work of accompaniment, I helped develop FORPP's Bogotá team in a big way. I discovered that I love the type of thinking that comes with figuring out what is working about an organization—and what could change to make it work better. I am really proud to say that there are parts of the organization that wouldn't have been the same without my input. Ultimately, it is not a job meant to last forever, and I have chosen to leave and do other things.

I've talked about confianza as a value, something knitted into the fabric of Colombian culture, and I do still think the country's happiness is wrapped up in that. In a bunch of places, among them some of the hottest parts of the country (conflict-wise), the happiest I've seen people is when there's a dance. (The double happiest I've seen people was when there was a dance with a live band.) In the campo, when people are happy, the night is filled with whooping. Even those few who don't dance like to watch. It's a break in the routine, and it's a mostly accepted way to share with many different people. There's no danger of armed actors, and the conflict is forgotten for a while.

When I asked Colombians, a few of them said that winning the World Cup would be a big morale booster. In 2014, it seemed like the whole country was yellow (the most prominent color of the

Colombian flag), and for many months after, the Cafeteros' breakout star, James Rodríguez, was everywhere, kissin' babies and otherwise blessing a slew of fun products.

The thing that makes me saddest/most uncomfortable about this is that it implies forgetting for a little while, rather than working through upset. But then again, this isn't about therapy, it's about happiness. So the happiness is in the dance.

But this idea—that a jolly trade could be made by sweeping the pain under the rug in order to let the nation's happiness preside— bothered me.

In general, people did seem pretty happy—yes, although the conflict has left no family untouched, has uprooted millions, and has created a basis for some true atrocities, there almost always is a place for lightness and laughter. Even in tense meetings, a joke about the heat, or lunch, would crack the tension, and everybody in the room conceded a small chuckle if not a hearty laugh, to my constant amazement.

Colombians have some pretty developed coping techniques, because to live with the heaviness of their reality would be debilitating otherwise.

If there's one thing that the Spanish-speaking world specializes in, it is memory, or remembrance, particularly with regard to those whose lives were taken by corrupt governments or twisted regimes. In all the memorial events, the message is clear: We remember those who are no longer here, we miss them, and we have to go on anyway. There was also a focus on the ultimate importance of truth with regard to the events that happened, in knowing that justice is being served. The question is whether the truth would be a relief or whether it would make everything even more painful. Is Colombia just plain happy? Or can Colombia be happy only when the truth is brought to light, with full knowledge that that will be painful and potentially unsatisfying? Is it worth it to create justice? What will make things better? How much and to what degree is Colombia's overall happiness wrapped up with its peace or relationship to its conflict?

I've started to better articulate my own definition of peace. In-country, there are signs with the national slogan campaigning for the peace agreements, reading, "*Yo soy la paz*" ("I am the peace"). It's interesting that they are using the singular rather than the plural. In a country in which solidarity is lived to such a degree that you always, always wait for people—but where confianza is key and not granted to everybody—I'm not sure which approach is a good one.

It's a common joke that when God was creating Colombia—Catholic country, people—God put all of these beautiful lands and rivers and creatures in the country and was asked, "Whoa! Won't that be too much for one place?" God winked and responded, "Just wait till you see the politics I put in there!"

"Colombia without conflict?" people say. "Can you imagine? It would be a paradise!"

I will no longer define peace as a lack of violence. I don't pretend to have a fully articulated vision of peace, but I'm working on uncovering it. I see peace as about building things, and creativity, and making communities that people have a space in and feel welcome to be a part of and can contribute to. Peace is about choice and play and enjoyment and about listening for the good, helpful, positive, or constructive in what people do. It is about belief in the value of forming things to be beautiful and taking the time to do so, and expressing what's important. And peace is about sharing.

It was a sobering return to the US, and in really unexpected moments, sometimes memories just popped up. The death of a great teacher and educator, Carlos Pedraza, who was killed after having disappeared for two days, affected me strongly.

I spent the summer in New Haven, Connecticut, working with teenagers making different kinds of art that they showed off at a little gallery toward the end of the session. I walked around laughing and hugging a new friend on staff as we took in all of the interesting pieces, until we came to a collaborative piece with three works held up on thin metal rods. The pieces were made of Barbies, and they were (left to right) a pair of legs extended wide, a torso, and I believe two arms all suspended there, labeled, "The Legs," "The Torso," "The Arms." Earlier in the session, human limbs had been found in town, and several days later the torso had been found separately. It obviously wasn't blatantly funny to people, but there was enough of a silliness factor, of independent limbs existing somewhere close. Clearly it was enough that our high schoolers were working through it consciously, enough that they made art about it.

I stopped and caught my breath, and felt that little feeling, like all of the blood in your body freezes for a few seconds before it remembers to go again, just a little chillier than before.

I had been totally taken by surprise and hugged my friend a little closer. It was a strange and somewhat beautiful coincidence that this friend had just returned from the Dominican Republic, doing work in a similar, politically hot region, where similar events can happen. In a moment where things were on the fast track for a serious emotional nosedive, we could feel a bit of a parachute open.

When I was in Colombia, the parts of the work I loved most were our acompañadxs and my fellow accompaniers, all of whom together were the most inspiration and support you can imagine. They were the best accompaniment during that perilous journey.

The question now is who will accompany me on my journey here at home. The answer, of course, is everyone who read my lengthy correspondence while I was in Colombia. I hope I told them how much I valued their support at the time, but perhaps I didn't say it clearly enough, or often enough, or loudly enough. So, for the record, I do thank them for being interested, for asking about or investigating my work. I offer a somewhat dumbfounded thank you to anyone who actually made it through all my emails. They were there when I was figuring things out. They were there for me even when they did not know it, when just thinking of them did so much to make me smile, remember, or giggle to myself. Their presence let me know that everything would be okay, including me. I'm usually pretty good at dealing with homesickness, but my electronic thumb-sucking (read: devices) were no replacement for getting to see my people, which I did eventually. (And for those I wasn't able to see, I know that our meeting will be an ecstatic adventure, whenever it happens!)

I'm taking time now to process it all. I continue to articulate what I want to take and what I want to be from this experience and am excitedly gathering materials and momentum before the next big professional move: to teaching high school Spanish at a charter school.

Those who accompanied me on this and other journeys—perilous and otherwise—are really the best. With gratitude, I offer them all my love.

Section Three

Home

Happiness, knowledge, not in another place
but this place—not for another hour, but this hour . . .

—WALT WHITMAN,
"CAROL OF OCCUPATIONS," LEAVES OF GRASS

MEG: It is always important to recognize the passions in ourselves and in our children, and find the ways to support that, even if not necessarily comfortable for us as parents. Of course, there needs to be balance with what we feel is important, and maybe even right, but we need to pay really close attention to these marvelous creatures who have come into our lives. Sometimes that means being willing to live with our own discomfort and theirs as they seek out what is important, discern what is essential, and when. Although it's ever so tempting to shoehorn our offspring into time frames that are convenient for us, it ultimately backfires in the most confounding and elaborate ways. Better to try to live with what is and make adjustments as necessary.

It felt like a homecoming to me when I read a passage in the novelist Maggie O'Farrell's recent memoir, *I Am, I Am, I Am*:

When *Alice's Adventures in Wonderland* was read to me
and Alice sighs, "Oh, how I long to run away from normal days! I want to run wild with my imagination," I
remember rising up from my pillow and thinking, "Yes,
yes, that's it exactly . . ." It was possible to ease this longing, to sate it. All I had to do was travel . . .

That unassailable flood of novelty, the stimulus of
uncharted territory, the overload of the unfamiliar, with
all synapses firing, connecting, signaling, burning new
pathways . . . I still crave the mental and physical jolt of
being somewhere new, of descending airplane steps into
a different climate, different faces, different languages.

Kate had loaned me O'Farrell's book while I was writing this one. I
don't think she had even considered the power of this particular passage, and how overwhelmingly relevant it felt. It's ironic that she passed
it on to me when my husband and I were visiting her and Chris, her
boyfriend, in Australia, where they were living and working for six
months before traveling in Southeast Asia for three months. Here we
were, living proof of the effect of the travel bug.

It was such a relief to read these words, to know that other people experience the kind of thirst that could only be quenched by time
in another culture, another climate, another way of living. The need
to explore, to be outside myself, stretching, learning, and just being.
Priceless and irreplaceable. I knew this to be true, yet it was not always
easy to create on a limited budget, and in particular with Duke's limited
budget of time off.

It became clear that I would need to do some of it on my own, as my
need was greater and my time a bit more flexible. Being my own boss

has distinct advantages, along with challenges, and this was certainly one of the upsides.

The whole notion became heightened and emphasized after my escapade with breast cancer. The year and a half of treatment did not keep me from doing a lot of things. I continued working and biking, doing laundry and pretending to put my wig on the cat. But we did not do a great deal of traveling, apart from visits to relatives. It became clear that it was still a priority, and in fact that its urgency was bumped up several notches. Even while anticipating a positive outcome, the sense of "Do it now" was clear and present.

I have always needed to balance all the things I want to do with what is possible at a particular time, and have learned that I can do much of what I like, just not all at the same time. I arrived at a place where priorities became more meaningful. What was really the advantage of waiting? It was a month following treatment that I visited Gale in Peru, and this proved just the right salve for my healing self. It was exciting and glorious to be there in and of itself, and just over the top to share the time with Gale. Thus began the first of the mother-daughter adventures.

I keep considering how travel affected my relationship with each of my daughters. I wish I could say that it changed the way we relate to each other. But in neither case was that obviously true. I strain to tease out the difference in the before and after but have failed to come up with anything specific.

In both cases it was nothing short of magical to explore new places. To spend time with Kate, making our way across the world to Nepal, was an adventure in the lavishness of extended time together. Out of our routine of home, and dropped into the unknown, it was a gift of untold proportions. It was both the spoken enjoyment of noticing the exotic scenes in Nepal and Bhutan, along with the companionable silences in between that added to the richness of our relationship. It was returning home with her and running into an absolute wall at 4 p.m. because of extreme jet lag. It was knowing that our relationship could continue to expand on the other side of the world. To be sure, it was also possible to become annoyed with each other, to have to work out each day's logistics, but these were also part of the fun (after the irritation subsided). Where would we find lunch? What was the most bizarre sight that day? It was an ongoing kaleidoscope of learning together.

To witness the grandeur of Machu Picchu with Gale was a dream. To be in Colombia, where she was making her temporary home, to meet the people she was interacting with, to be on the ground where she was taking in unfathomable amounts of information and working to keep people safe created a bond that will always remain. What else is there in life besides sharing space, time, thoughts, feelings, and love with those who mean the very most to you?

There are times when we cannot rush an outcome. We cannot always know what the options are. Sometimes we need to sit with the yoke of uncertainty, because there is no other choice. But when we hold all the cards and the only obstacle to moving forward is our tether to the familiar, it is time to support the need for connection to the world, to the unfamiliar and all the untold treasures and mysteries it promises to divulge.

This notion was never something I shared explicitly with my children. I didn't sit them down and lay it out as a critical life skill. Although I'm aware that children learn so much by osmosis, I could not have predicted how deeply they would take in this aspect of life, each in a different way, but powerfully nonetheless. I shouldn't have been surprised when as teenagers they both started making noises about visiting other countries and planning ways to accomplish their travel goals.

Although their assumptions about the ease and accessibility of travel were understandably different from my own (as they had come of age in the world of Google Maps, deregulated airlines, and Airbnb), we all shared an understanding that connection—to ourselves, to each other, to the world around us—is the whole point. The more we know ourselves, the easier it is to connect with others, and the more connected we are with others, the easier it is to be at home in our own skin. Each connection spirals out to other people in the world, making larger circles and encompassing ever more.

I believe that we must fan the flames of curiosity and adventure in our own children. They may make different choices, they may seek out adventures we might never have fathomed. And isn't that part of the treat of parenting? To see our children's horizons broaden in the most authentic way? To experience new things with them, and to watch as they help others welcome something new?

The goal is not to avoid the scary. The goal is to make smaller what appears to be scary, and to scaffold confidence and curiosity to deal with the difficult. It is to know that the connection to self will determine when it is time to venture out and when it is time to come home. The key is to know yourself, your passions, and where your balance lies.

And how did this passion of mine take root in the first place?

I grew up in the Hudson Valley of New York State. The son of Russian immigrants, my dad was a classically trained, Juilliard-educated oboist and pianist. An unexpected stint with Charlie Parker in order to make money to court my mom in his early twenties rocked (or jazzed up) his world. He started SUNY (State University of New York) New Paltz's jazz program, which still exists today. My mom started a preschool and kindergarten in a serendipitous partnership that lasted for twenty-five years.

I studied piano and violin growing up, but fortunately, my parents did not demand that I continue my music studies. I loved music and still do, but it was clear that I lacked the discipline and drive to pursue it professionally.

My dad worried about my hands and fingers when I began skiing and horseback riding. I was an active child, playing neighborhood kickball and touch football, and riding my bike everywhere: to the tennis courts, friends' houses, and work.

I grew up during a time when it was fine to be out most of the day and to return for fuel before heading back out. I took full advantage, enjoying the group of kids who lived within a radius of a few blocks. My parents placed a fair amount of trust in my judgment, and I was probably given even more freedom when their attention was devoted to my sister, who was diagnosed with a learning disability in high school.

Once I was a teenager, I didn't give them reason to doubt their loose reins. I didn't need oversight with homework (although I did need reminders about practicing), and I loved nights spent ice-skating on the pond with friends, going out to hear music on weekends, and getting into bars at age sixteen.

When my parents pursued therapy for themselves and my sister—in the process educating me about this type of treatment—they read my freedom as complete independence, and they would sometimes assert, "You'll never need therapy!"

I'm now a trained social worker and clinical psychotherapist. Fortunately, en route to getting there, I was able to overcome this declaration. I see mental health treatment as something that should be as readily accessible as treatment for physical health. If it were provided in the same way, perhaps people would be able to avail themselves of counseling much sooner—and depression, anxiety, and stress could be much less of a threat to people's health.

But at the time, it was likely easier for them to see me as self-sufficient and capable, and not to consider that I could also be vulnerable.

My parents' first foray into international travel came with their six-week trip to Europe when I was thirteen. My trip to Besançon, France, the summer I turned fifteen would shift my worldview, setting the stage for a semester in Aix-en-Provence.

It all fed my ravenous appetite to know more about the beauty and the people that populated the planet. After college, I traveled across the States on my own, winding up in San Francisco, where I lived for a year. Next was England for eight months, before returning for graduate school in Boston, my travel appetite temporarily sated.

It was several years after this that Duke and I began our own journey together.

When Duke and I started dating, we lived almost four hours apart, no matter which route we took. It quickly became obvious to me that the only path to sanity was to listen to good music while I drove.

"I need to buy a car stereo," I declared after six weeks. The purchase would be a major chunk of change, but it felt like a vital investment.

Duke's eyes lit up. Electronics: Hell, yeah!

"Great!" he said. "I'll install it for you!" But on the way home from the mall, Duke glanced over at me and was startled to see tears making their way down my cheeks. "What is it?" he asked anxiously.

At first, all I could do was shake my head. But when I saw him struggling to sort out what these TUOs (tears of unknown origin) meant, I smiled.

"I'm happy," I explained. I could see that this explanation wasn't landing. So I tried again: "I would not be buying this stereo if this thing we have going wasn't a *really* big deal."

Duke took my hand and exhaled in relief. "It seemed like this was a fun purchase. I couldn't imagine what had gone wrong." He smiled and gave my hand a squeeze.

And just like that, we were unofficially engaged.

You may be wondering: "Where's Duke in these stories?"

The simple answer is that he has never been as keen on travel as the rest of us, but he participated enthusiastically in every trip that I conjured. The reality of his work schedule means that getting away for more than a week at a time can be tricky.

I would have loved for him to join us, and I understood that there was a part of him that felt left out of our adventures. I did not want to give up opportunities to travel, even if it meant that Duke could not take part. That would have bred too much resentment on my part. Accommodating our differences is a part of our commitment to each other and to the dynamic nature of our relationship.

There is no perfect equation that fits all couples, and no pair glides along like dolphins in perfect synchronicity. There's always the risk that adjustment might be too burdensome for one party. But it's still necessary for the health and growth of a relationship.

I see this over and over in my work as a therapist. In order to make this kind of assessment more impartial and less judgmental, I sometimes ask my clients to describe themselves and their partner as animals.

One client couple agreed that the female partner was a cat. She liked a lot of time alone. She was quiet and introverted, and she did not like to be disturbed.

She saw her spouse as a lion who roared and was strong, dominating, fierce, loyal. But he saw himself as a working dog, like a Saint Bernard or a sheepdog, someone who liked to keep busy.

This divergence perfectly encapsulated the disconnect between them. She was intimidated by his naturally loud voice and impatience. But he was just on the go, trying to get things done. In the framework of the exercise, both could see that he was not intending to be larger than life. I could see the relief on her face.

"I actually think you're a handsome lion," she offered.

"Well, I like that very much," he responded. The tension had drained out of the conversation, and a new way forward was beginning.

Duke and I also negotiate to make room for what the other needs. (When it comes to our own animal assessment, I am for sure a dog, wagging my tail, eager to play. He is a cat, looking for company at certain times.)

Understanding his background helps make sense of his attitude toward travel. Duke grew up in a family that traveled much more than mine. His father was lit up by meeting Sargent Shriver in the early 1960s. He ditched his career selling computers for IBM in order to become deputy director of the Peace Corps in Ghana and Liberia, moving the entire family there for two years when his two sons were young. Duke was enrolled in seven schools before the fifth grade.

His father went on to a career in high-level government and UN positions for ten years, culminating later in life as deputy high commissioner for refugees in Geneva. He was frequently out of the country for work.

We met during his father's only stint in academia. Their family had moved to New Paltz, New York, where my dad was teaching college-level music. We had family friends in common during the two years that Duke's family lived there, and we saw each other very occasionally in the years after. Notably, we crossed paths on that lovely day in Los Angeles when I tried to keep up with Mr. Roller Skater.

But then, when we were both almost twenty-nine, Duke ensured that I received an invitation to his brother's wedding.

I was smitten with the red-haired and bearded guy in the tuxedo, and people noticed that he spent much of the night dancing with the woman in the lavender dress.

Two weeks later, I decided to take a few days off between jobs to visit a friend, and I called Duke to see if he could put me up on my way there. I later learned that he looked around his studio apartment, considered that he lived only fifteen minutes from my parents' house, where I could have chosen to stay instead—and responded with an emphatic YES.

One night turned into two, plus a visit on my way back. After that, we alternated making that three-hour-and-forty-five-minute drive, which led to the car stereo purchase with my happy tears, our (actual) engagement, Gale and Kate, and our thirty-fourth anniversary, which we celebrated in 2021.

When we make the commitment to marry, we do so from where we are at that moment. The better we know ourselves, the more likely we are to know what we're looking for in a partner, and the better we're able to calculate the risk about what life might look like in the future.

But of course, we cannot know what surprises we'll encounter. Could Duke have predicted that I would want to go off and explore? Could he have known how much effort it might take for him to get away with me? Would that have been a game changer, or would it have altered our trajectory if he had known for sure up front?

Certainly, there were clues early on that I loved travel—after all, we reconnected when I was on a solo cross-country trip. At twenty-two, neither of us was in a position to make any commitments or had any desire to. I was all about exploring, moving, learning. Duke was involved in working with his brother and partying. Neither of us had a clear direction. It would be several more years before we would both be ready to settle down.

Working out the travel thing took some doing. He completely understood that I wanted to see Gale in Peru just a month after all my treatments for breast cancer. (I could probably have asked for anything at that point and he would have agreed.) He understood my need for subsequent trips as well, but these did not always sit well, in part for financial reasons.

How much should I limit myself, if Duke was not able or willing to go on a trip? Should I hold back? Would I restrain my own yearning because he was not making the choice to pursue it?

I knew I would feel deep resentment if I did not capitalize on opportunities when they presented themselves. Once some trains leave the station, they are not returning. While I could appreciate Duke's hesitation or resistance, I did not want it to shut down my own longing. Ultimately, he understood my need to scratch my itchy feet and not to resent it.

We can commit to direct conversation and openness, knowing that not everyone will always be thrilled with every outcome. But it is still important to put all the possibilities on the table. It is here where compromise becomes a real thing, not a given, and it requires generosity and the expanse of love to create space for the relationship to breathe and grow.

Who will accompany you on this vast and varied odyssey? Who will be there across this landscape steep and broad?

We can choose some of our wonderful companions. (Some might argue that we choose them all according to need at the time.) Certainly, some are placed in our path, and some wind up part of our life's thread. Others show up for snippets: a train ride, a class, a project.

We can't always know who those people will be. Will that dear high school friend still feel connected after college? Will the college friend still relate after children—or without them? When we choose a partner, how certain are we that the union will withstand the rigors of life's rapids?

There are no guarantees, even within a family. We hope that the bonds will remain steadfast, dependable, resilient. But we cannot know what will challenge our links.

We can only make sure that we tend to our own gentle stalks—not only our children, but also our friends, our mates, our family. We can ensure that our hearts are open to receive and to give.

Not a simple task, or a one-time event, but we can create the opportunities: the car rides to and from school, the dinners created and shared, the coffee in bed, the card sent to someone who has suffered a loss, the hikes to the mountaintops small and large.

Every close relationship has a bank of goodwill. When we make a deposit—by spending time together, doing small favors, celebrating occasions, or taking a walk together—the balance grows. In the event of a small misunderstanding, an account withdrawal doesn't hurt too much. If, however, the relationship is close to bankrupt, then any withdrawal can threaten to disrupt the bond. It's vital for both members to consciously make deposits, keeping the balance as healthy as possible.

Providence deposits people in our path, and it is up to us to choose how we nourish and cultivate those relationships. I consider the timeline of my life, and the people who have been present and co-created my story, my journey, my time on the earth.

My parents provided a stable place for me to stretch, the clear knowledge that I was loved and could try out my own way of being, and the confidence to make my own effective choices, or to learn from the ones that are less so. I become overwhelmed when I consider the chain of people, the village that sustained my childhood and beyond.

Never was the importance of interdependence as great as during my treatment for breast cancer. Being stubbornly independent, I learned quickly how vital it was to not only accept the assistance of others, but to honor and respect it for the gift that it invariably was. Every dinner, every flower, every card offered a warm hand, a blessing, and a connection robed in love.

I reflect on the woman who made me dinner when I was in France for the semester. She showed me that even though I was there only for a short while, I could find people to enjoy and feel comfortable with.

The young men on our Nepal hike shared their stories, their company, and their music, all of which were important during that long climb.

The woman occupying the corner house in Gale's Colombian community offered her home and a generous meal without having met me before.

My clients unfold their secrets and their willingness to look inside themselves. They take the risk of allowing me to really hear them, but also to consider my words and thoughts.

My husband willingly entered into our relationship, knowing that I am a committed punster who needs to roam, climb, ride, and sing. He signed on, taking the deep dive. I push him out of his comfort zone at times, to places unfamiliar, to people he may not have otherwise met. He pushes my sense of art, forces me to articulate when I am not feeling settled and when I need help.

And of course, we partnered to bring two magnificent beings into the world. Sometimes life's balance felt like a row of spinning plates, with us running to keep them all in motion. But other times we had the luxury of a gambol on the beach or a gaze at the galaxy.

Gale and Kate, who did not necessarily request to be accompanied by us (or did they?) entered our lives with a grace and a gusto that at times leaves me breathless, at times awestruck, but always profoundly grateful to have these creative, compassionate, adventurous souls present for our shared spin on earth.

Who will we accompany? We cannot always know. But we can hold them close when they are near, so we can still hold them when they are far. With arms outstretched, from here to there, connected we go.

Acknowledgments

WHO HAS ACCOMPANIED me on this leg of the journey? The sprawling city that helped birth this baby is so diverse, generous, and talented.

I will start with Joan Borysenko, who helped plant the seedling of this story by reminding me that every book has its own path and that no two follow the same route.

Susan Barraco, my first editor, helped move my ideas from mosaic to extended mural.

Samantha Shubert, with her super editing power, patiently helped shape this story, so that all the parts connected.

My beta readers—Ryan Ruopp, Anne Estes, Mer McCauley, and Jennifer Whitney—braved the first complete draft, and each offered comments that strengthened the story.

And of course, my family has been involved at every step. Gale and Kate, this is only part of a love letter to you. It has been my profound delight to be with you anywhere in the world. Thank you for bearing with me through the seemingly unending editing process. And Duke, my loving home base and travel companion, thank you for listening to pieces of this, and for accompanying me on this circuitous and kaleidoscopic journey called life.

Author Q&A

Q: When did you first get the thought that you would write a book about your travels with your daughters? How did it evolve?

A: It wasn't long after I returned from the trip to Nepal and Bhutan that I thought it would be interesting to see side by side the observations that Kate and I made during that trip. There was a strongly meditative aspect to each of our travels, but also a number of striking differences, starting with our divergent life stages, and the fact that she was sitting, and I was hiking. In fact, the very first iteration of the book was called *Sitting on Top of the World*. But it wasn't sitting right (so to speak) and in a teary revelation, I knew that the book needed to include Gale's time in Colombia and my visit with her there. It was a circuitous loop taking the whole thing apart and putting it back together by topic and then taking it apart again and reattaching it chronologically.

As with our children, we have some say in how we shape a book, but they really take on their own lives and we have to be careful not to impose too much of our own sensibilities on them. It's that balance of observing and seeing what's there with infusing bits of ourselves.

Q: When did you first become interested in writing, and how did that interest develop?

A : I started writing as a tot when I would make tiny books and tape or staple them together at age three. My mother prided herself on allowing me to sound out words I didn't know how to spell, so writing has been in my blood for a way long time.

I took off time to write after my first job as a clinical social worker. I wasn't earning enough money writing and working for a caterer, so I returned to the field of social work. My column writing took hold then, but my first book didn't appear until after I wrote about my jaunt with breast cancer: My email distribution updates seemed to really speak to people, and they even tolerated (or encouraged) my pun compulsion. After a number of people encouraged me to get the updates into book form, they were eventually edited into *Topic of Cancer: Riding the Waves of the Big C.* That was a very exciting thing, and I didn't know then that my next book would come out just over ten years later.

Q : Can you talk a bit about your writing process? How do you get in the mood to write? Do you have any writing rituals?

A : My columns usually start to write themselves in my head as I bicycle my variety of 20–35-mile loops. When I get back, I write them out with pen and paper because I love the physical act of writing, and it's a powerful way to download thoughts. The words go through a filter on their way from brain to paper. Next, I type them into the computer and do some editing there. Then I print them out, correct errors, and read them out loud, usually to my husband if he is home. If not, the dogs and cat are not judgmental.

Because my full-time focus has been my psychotherapy practice, my writing needs have to work around it. This may change when I start working less in a few years and have more time to develop stories. Time will tell.

Q : You write: "It will take some time to fully appreciate what we have brought home from the mountains and streets of Kathmandu and Bhutan." Since some time has now gone by, what do you more fully appreciate about what you learned on this journey and in Colombia?

A : Being in Kathmandu was humbling because nothing replaces seeing and feeling the struggles that people experience to drive home the point that it shouldn't have to be that way. Luck plays such a big role in our placement on Earth. Certainly, the way we choose to live our lives matters, but the cards we are dealt determine a lot about what some of those options are. It takes strength, courage, and support to be able to see clearly beyond our perceived limitations and take steps toward something that is unknown or abstract.

In contrast to all that was the *unimaginable splendor* of the Himalayas. Their size and strength touched the core of my being, and just walking around them was filling and nourishing in a way I had never experienced before. I was also drawn to the overlay of religions and how the way that people view their respective religions not only greatly informs their lives, but also how they interact with other people. It always fascinates me when people hold points of view or beliefs that are so different from my own, and I am drawn to understand what makes people do what they do. That's part of why I am still practicing psychotherapy. I am endlessly curious about how people arrive at the decisions they make and how we can learn to listen to ourselves more clearly to expand the range of choices we believe are available to us.

The lush countryside of Colombia is stunning and teeming with life and possibility. The range of fruits and food mirrors the palpable passion of the Colombian people for where and who they are. I saw only a tiny portion of this country, but I was aware of the shadow of the displaced people, how it happens to friends and loved ones, and how the domestic conflict results in such a vast amount of energy being spent in such a draining way. I don't have to wonder whether I will come under attack if I just go out to a routine doctor's appointment. Living with the backdrop of this kind of threat is wearing in ways those people won't completely understand until it is no longer present.

Q : Kate wrote, "I'm really leaning on the theories that meditation brings happiness and that challenge brings happiness." What are your own personal thoughts on how to achieve happiness?

A : I believe that one of the keys is in really being present. It's an ongoing challenge and requires being willing to let in what is actually happening and honoring whatever response I have to that. It's not easy, but the reward is big, and it's a simple way to live. In addition, I know I need enough exercise, time with my family and friends, enough time to play and be entertained, and sufficient time in beautiful places. Good food, compelling reading, spending enough time near animals all contribute to my happiness.

Doing work that I love and that makes me think or expands my view are all key. It's a hell of a spicy salad, this life thing. And an ever-shifting balance. We have to keep paying attention to the way it morphs in order to stay in a good place. That's the challenge and that's the fun. So many opportunities and possibilities. They're endless.

Q : Can you discuss how you may have changed as a parent after your adventures?

A : In both cases I was struck by my daughters' competence and growth. They think for themselves and are ever learning about where they are, who they are, and what that combination brings. In both cases it was a reminder to support them and enjoy the process of their evolution.

Q : You alluded to the fact that you found it somewhat difficult to enter the empty-nest stage of life. What advice do you have or did you get on raising children?

A : It's important always to have parts of our lives that are our own. Fortunately, we have the advantage of our children growing up and out gradually, so we are slowly introduced to the notion of our lives remaining entwined, but with a much looser hold.

Traveling with Gale and Kate meant lots of hours together—the fun, the annoying, the boring. In some ways traveling together made it more difficult when they were out of the house completely because I missed being with them, but in others, it made it easier because it created a tangible glue that will always be there. It's a dynamic process. Relationships don't end, but they do change shape over time.

My parents always encouraged me to do well in school, and for the most part left me to it. My dad, in particular, really emphasized that I should work really hard, but never so hard that I didn't leave enough time to enjoy myself. I so appreciate this sense of balance.

In terms of money, again passed from my parents, I feel responsible about my bills and am never behind, but always try to remember that money is to be enjoyed, especially with those I love. Money absolutely reflects a sense of priorities, and sometimes doing one certain thing means something else has to wait. My parents always had cars that worked fine but were not fancy. (Toyota Corolla, VW Bug) They chose instead to go to the theater and concerts. I put all my funds towards travel in my early twenties (surprise!), when some friends were saving for houses or furniture. Priorities shifted with marriage, children, etc. We have never had a lot of money, but I have never felt deprived. The girls seem to have absorbed this and are able to find ways to fund the activities that are important. They are both creative and careful about how they buy clothing, furniture, concert tickets, and plane tix!

Q: What other hobbies do you have besides traveling and writing?

A: I love to bicycle and hike. I also love to swim, walk the dogs, do Zumba, and of course EAT! My husband and I both enjoy cooking when we have the time. He bakes bread (and I steal the heels). It's always fun to find new restaurants, and we also LOVE hearing live music, which we miss because of the pandemic. Reading is a treat, and getting outside in the winter means using skis, snowshoes, or just warm boots to walk in the woods.

Q: Now that you have completed this book, what are your next major goals?

A: I LOVE writing my (now monthly) columns which I have been doing for almost forty years now on a huge variety of topics. I would love to have them organized by category and gathered together in book form. Beyond that, I haven't begun to conceive of my next book.

Q : Do you have an update on other travel adventures your daughters and/or you have taken or plan to take?

A : Kate moved to London in September of 2021 to attend a two-year graduate course in Human Development, focusing on early childhood. Gale doesn't have specific plans at the moment, but I can see her feet itching and know that it's just a matter of time before she plots her next adventure. I bicycled from Boston to New York in October 2021 (delayed from 2020) and plan to hike around Mont Blanc in 2022. I'm sure I will plan other trips as time and health (mine and that of the world) allows. Who knows where the compass may point beyond that, and what combination of hearty souls will be my traveling companions?

About the Authors

MEG STAFFORD is a writer who loves exploration of all kinds. Her 2011 memoir, *Topic of Cancer: Riding the Waves of the Big C*, won six literary awards (including being named Best First Book by the IBPA's Benjamin Franklin Awards) for its engrossing and hilarious portrayal of surviving and thriving after a life-altering diagnosis of breast cancer. For twenty-five years she has been observing how small, remarkable moments enrich our lives in her monthly newspaper column, "A Moment's Notice." As a social worker in private practice, she's been helping others negotiate the terrain of relationships and connections for over thirty-five years. She lives in Massachusetts with her husband, two dogs, and one large cat.

GALE STAFFORD has been teaching high school Spanish in Massachusetts since 2016. She continues to pursue her love of dance, seeks out musical performances of all types, and attentively develops her skill in making colorful handmade pasta. She is considering her next pursuits, both professionally and in her top places to explore, including Oaxaca, Reykjavik, and Wellington.

KATE STAFFORD has returned to the UK to study Developmental Psychology at University College London, based at the Anna Freud Centre for Children and Families. Her passion for Ultimate Frisbee led her to captain her team's championship at University in Edinburgh. She will undoubtedly visit more of the surrounding countries over the next several years.